Infinite AWAKENING

A Miraculous Journey for the Advanced Soul

JASON CHAN

and

JANE ROGERS

Grosvenor House
Publishing Limited

The right of Jason Chan and Jane Rogers to be identified as the author of this
work has been asserted in accordance with Section 78
of the Copyright, Designs and Patents Act 1988

The book cover picture is copyright to Jason Chan and Jane Rogers

This book is published by
Grosvenor House Publishing Ltd
28-30 High Street, Guildford, Surrey, GU1 3EL.
www.grosvenorhousepublishing.co.uk

A CIP record for this book
is available from the British Library

ISBN 978-1-78148-392-3

ACKNOWLEDGMENTS

First and foremost, we would like to thank all those awakening individuals who have listened to Jason's enlightening spiritual talks over many years. Without you, this book could never have been written!

Next, we would like to thank Carole Atman, Louise Rabour and Gloria Hanson for their wonderful editing and proof reading of this book.

Finally we extend our heart-felt thanks to Irina Popova for designing the book cover and to Monika Witkowska who took the photograph of Jason Chan for the front cover.

INTRODUCTION

We thank you for picking up or downloading this book.

Our heartfelt wish is that reading this book and practising the meditations at the end of each chapter will assist you to awaken to the miraculous truth about your extremely precious existence.

We know that most human beings find life on this planet pretty challenging, but we are convinced that there is a way to lead truly loving, peaceful, joy-filled lives here, and we are determined to help as many people as we can to find it.

The rest of the book is written as though Jason Chan were talking to you. In fact, it was written by Jane Rogers who transcribed and then edited a series of spiritual talks that Jason gave in a wide range of settings over many years. Jane has adapted these talks so that even if you have never met Jason, nor attended any of his courses or retreats, you can still tune into his unique spiritual teachings.

Please feel absolutely free to disagree with or disregard anything in this book that does not sit well with you. We are definitely not trying to convert you to any particular form of spirituality. We simply want you to progress as far as you possibly can this lifetime down your own unique path of infinite awakening and self-healing. We wish you great happiness and fulfilment in your life, and truly believe that the spiritual principles and practices described in this book may speed you on your way to attaining them.

CONTENTS

Chapter One

The Call to Awake

Awakening is a Must

This book begins with a loving call to you:

'Awake now while you still have the chance!'

The core purpose of *Infinite Awakening* is to assist you to free yourself from the suffering of normal human existence. In this book, I will share with you some of the key spiritual practices that will enable you to awaken from a fearful dream created by relatively low levels of consciousness into a much higher state of consciousness that is always filled with love and light.

Do you realise that you are basically living out a bad dream and that deep down, you are so lonely and dissatisfied with life that however hard you try, you can never find the lasting love and happiness you seek? Consciously or subconsciously, you are trapped by a tragic belief that you are unworthy of love. You then keep trying to fill up your deep sense of lack and loneliness by attempting to get what you think you need from the world around you. For example, you may try to attract someone who appears to have certain qualities you lack, and then attempt to cling onto them, in order to feel more complete. In modern society, we even call this behaviour 'falling in love'.

On the other hand, you may well dislike those who remind you of your own deep sense of unworthiness, and then insist they are 'the guilty ones' who deserve to be punished, rather than you.

You look fearfully out into the world around you and see others as attackers, whilst you are their innocent victim.

After a long, long time of playing this guilt tripping game – without, of course, realising you are doing it – your mind has become choc-a-bloc with stored grievances against the world. You are convinced the external world is to blame for your unhappiness, or pain. Even if you have been on a spiritual path for quite some time, you may notice that you still have a very strong tendency to blame others, or external circumstances beyond your control, for your continuing dissatisfaction with life.

You probably believe that you have an independent mind and that you are intelligent enough to work out how to be successful in life. I do not doubt for one second that you are highly intelligent and well-educated, but I still have to tell you that your thinking mind has been programmed and so it is now primarily working against you, instead of for you.

Throughout your formative years, you acquired a lot of toxic beliefs, such as, 'Men cannot be trusted,' or 'Women are two-faced.' Today the media, and indeed the collective consciousness of all those around you, influence you with negative beliefs, such as 'Right-wing politicians are greedy and selfish,' or 'Socialists are dangerous, loony-lefties.' Programmed beliefs such as these now run much of your life. This may all sound terribly dark and gloomy, and even preposterous, to you, but I am sure you will at least agree that your life up to now has not been one long bed of roses and that you sometimes despair of ever finding the lasting peace and fulfilment you so long for.

Well, this book is designed to assist you in finding lasting love and happiness by pointing the way back home to a heavenly state of consciousness. In later chapters, I will show you how to progress step by step down a genuine spiritual path that we will call 'The Path of Infinite Awakening'. Not many people in our world are consciously choosing to follow an awakening path like this yet, but the momentum of a collective awakening of human kind is certainly gathering pace. In any case, awakening is a choiceless choice all human beings will make sooner or later, as their consciousness expands beyond the purely physical level of existence and they begin to see a much bigger picture that reflects the absolute truth about life. So why not lead the way and commit to becoming a pioneer of awakened living?

This Book is Addressed to Your Soul

When I lovingly urge you to awake this lifetime, please understand that I am addressing your core-being rather than your personality-self. I know that your personality-self seems totally real to you, but I have to tell you, from a spiritual perspective, your personality-self is just a temporary dream-figure stuck in the middle of a frightening dream. Meanwhile, your true-self, which we might call your soul, is trapped in fear and darkness because you have completely forgotten about it, and thus left it imprisoned in a mind constantly dreaming a fearful dream.

You may have no idea why life seems to be so difficult and painful and why lasting peace and happiness seem almost impossible for you to attain. But the miraculously good news I want to share with you, is that there is a way for your soul to escape from this nightmare, and in this book, I will reveal some of the secrets of this eternal escape route to you.

But please note, you may not like everything I am about to tell you because we all have a lot of resistance to following any truly awakening path. Genuine spiritual teachings are not for our personalities. *A Course in Miracles,* for example, is not a manual for leading a highly successful normal life. It is not a grander version of *The Secret!* But, if you are a serious spiritual seeker, sooner or later, your longing to liberate your soul will become stronger than your personality's search for the 'good life'.

However, please do not make the common mistake of believing that any genuine path to enlightenment is a path of renunciation, or of sacrifice. This is a very outdated idea. One of the wonderful side effects of following a genuine path of enlightenment is that you will begin to dream a much happier dream, full of enduring love and joy.

I sincerely hope you will create a truly successful life for yourself. But I do have to tell you, having a relatively good normal life is still unsatisfactory and painful. Even billionaires, for example, still have relationship problems, and they will still age, get sick and die.

Unfortunately, intellectually understanding human suffering is not enough to lead us out of it. Whether you realise it yet or not, you are desperate to escape from the prison of ordinary human consciousness. You are longing to escape all the pain, confusion and loneliness of unawakened human existence. But the only fool-proof way to make this escape is to follow a path of spiritual empowerment that will lift your consciousness way up above all of your painful past programming. You need to do this, not only to discover the incredible love and light at the core of your being, but also to assist the whole of humankind to evolve into lasting love, peace and joy.

Last century, human beings killed hundreds of millions of their own kind. So far this century, we may have killed fewer people, but we are still pretty aggressive as a species. What on earth is going so wrong? We are not doing well collectively or individually, despite being the most intelligent species on the planet. Isn't it now finally time for us to raise our consciousness up to the level of unconditional love and light? Wouldn't you love to connect to a higher wisdom that can lead all of us out of the mindset of endless scarcity, fear and conflict? Don't you long to greet a new dawn for humankind, filled with love and light, and imbued with lasting peace and beauty? If so, you and I have no more time to waste.

If you believe that you still have plenty of time down here on earth to pursue a variety of goals both worldly and spiritual, you are in denial. One lifetime is extremely short, and if you think you have all the time in the world to awake, you are like an ostrich burying its head in the sand. Please do not be an ostrich. Become a wise owl, and realise that the unique opportunity we have to awake and to heal in this lifetime is incredibly precious.

Attaining lasting spiritual enlightenment is not an easy goal to fulfil. It can seem like 'Mission Impossible', because we have to undo so many layers of egoic programming. To date, only a handful of spiritual geniuses have ever totally transcended all of this programming. Basically, the obstacles we face on the path to enlightenment, or complete self-realisation, are almost insurmountable, without some kind of miraculous higher assistance. The really good news however is that higher assistance is always totally available to us the moment we genuinely ask to receive it.

If you are reading this, I would hazard a guess you are no longer simply sleep-walking through your life. You are seeking for truth, and as part of that search, you have picked up this book. Moreover, you may well have volunteered to come down to earth to complete a unique spiritual mission, possibly in conjunction with other members of your soul group.

A number of mature souls are reincarnating into a physical body once again at this stage in our human evolution because they have a soul contract to fulfil this lifetime. Before they were born, some souls even agreed they would awaken this lifetime and then team up with other advanced souls to assist them to awake and heal too.

It is most likely that you are one of these mature souls. But please be patient. Do not be in too much of a rush to save the world, or you may just end up making even more of a mess. Some individuals may need to follow an awakening path for a number of years, before their soul's true purpose this lifetime is fully revealed to them.

Mature souls who volunteer for a mission to planet earth already have all the qualities that they need to complete their mission. However, because the energy and collective consciousness of humankind is still relatively low, it can take enormous effort to remember why they came down here in the first place, and even more effort to cultivate the worldly skills they will need to fulfil their soul's mission this lifetime.

According to *A Course in Miracles*, you are the perfect child of God, but I guess that you may not be fully aware of your true identity yet. You may still be driven mad from time to time by your unfulfilled desire for a piece of chocolate, a cold beer, sex, or a break from the stress of your daily life. You may still get really irritated or upset when another personality makes a disparaging remark about you. All this keeps happening because you have forgotten your true identity. Please do not feel guilty or disheartened about this. You are just a paid-up member of the human race, and being fearful and grumpy is a requirement for membership.

Meditation as a Key Awakening Practice

None of us can transcend all of our painful desires and aversions without raising our consciousness up to the level of unconditional love and light. But for centuries, the Western world has lacked the knowledge of powerful meditation practices that can assist us to cut through all of the conflict and darkness in our own minds so that we can become aware of the infinite love that is our eternal essence.

If you ask me, 'Can I get enlightened without a serious meditation practice of some kind?' I would have to say 'No', because your ordinary, thinking mind simply will not allow you to know the truth. Can you be a very helpful, kind person without meditating? Of course you can, but sadly, many incredibly kind, helpful people still suffer terribly in this world.

Some people believe that if they are very good, they will go to heaven after they die. But I have to tell you that after you die, you do not suddenly turn into an angel perching on a fluffy white cloud in heaven. Basically, you stay the same person you are now, but minus your physical body. However, whilst you still have a physical existence, you do have a miraculous opportunity to transcend at least some of your current weaknesses and grievances and to further cultivate your unique talents and gifts.

So whatever you do, please do not choose an unawakened life. A life like this is pretty meaningless and lonely, because basically nobody else really cares that much about your life and no one can completely share it with you. They are all far too busy worrying about themselves.

I do not want to shatter your illusions, but not even your 'soul mate', or 'twin flame', can share your feelings, or alleviate all of your deep inner pain and loneliness. Basically, you live your whole life alone, even if there happens to be another warm, attractive body sleeping next to yours every night, because you can never totally join with someone through the body. You can only completely join with another being soul to soul, and to do this, you first have to be awake.

Please do not insist that you are currently too busy to stop and devote at least some of your time to your spiritual awakening. Be brave and decide that you are going to plan a daring escape from human suffering. Then commit to following your unique path out of suffering and into true love for as long as it takes.

If you commit the whole of the rest of your life to your own awakening and healing, I can assure you that you will be among the most blessed and fulfilled human beings on the planet. You will also become a radiant pioneer in human evolution; a shining example for other human beings to follow.

Changing Your Mind

To awake to the miraculous truth about life, you do not have to sell your house, leave your family, shave your head, or move to a mountaintop in Tibet. You just have to change your mind. Is awakening really that simple? On one level, yes it is. All suffering and all happiness lie in your own mind. This is a universal truth. Therefore, if you are suffering, or longing to lead a more fulfilling life, you have to change your mind and turn away from living in a fearful dream, to dwell in the truth and nothing but the truth. How do you do this? You do it by going on an incredible inner journey that will take you back home to love.

We all try so hard to be happy, but most of the time, we are not. The majority of human beings are just dreaming their lives away. They argue with their loved ones. They hate their work, or spend most of their working lives longing for a holiday. They wake up feeling anxious and go to sleep feeling worn out. What sort of life is this?

But to begin to awake, you can simply ask yourself, 'What is my life for?' 'Why am I here and where am I going?' You then need to find the answer to these crucial questions. But your thinking brain cannot answer these questions for you. Only your intuitive heart knows the real purpose of your life.

So many people try to create some kind of meaningful purpose for their life. Most modern Westerners no longer believe in a God who has a divine purpose for them, and so they now create a purpose for their life from the work they do, or from raising a family. However, there is definitely a much deeper universal purpose to life that makes our physical existence truly meaningful, and that purpose is to awake and to heal our deluded minds and broken hearts, so we can return home to infinite love and infinite freedom.

This is your soul's true purpose, but you will not be able to see it, until you raise your consciousness and sharpen your perception. Then, and only then, can you begin to bypass your thinking brain and connect to that spark of light, or life, deep within you that is longing to be dwelling in love, and nothing but love, eternally.

Following Your Heart

Your thinking brain, however intelligent it is, is not a 'knowing' mechanism. It is basically a programmed machine. So please don't ask your brain how to awake to the ultimate truth about life. It will not give you any useful answers. Don't ask your mind how to find a genuine path to enlightenment. Just follow the deep calling of your heart.

Long before you begin to awake consciously, your heart already knows what is for your highest good. Your heart will sing with joy when you make any decision that is aligned with your soul's highest purpose in life. So please always follow your heart. Just do what makes your heart sing, rather than what your logical mind tells you to do.

Some advanced souls may need to become singers or writers to spread the light. Others may have to become spiritual teachers, or healers of some kind. It may take you several years of awakening before you know exactly how you are going to fulfil your soul's unique purpose this lifetime, but if you continue to ignore the ceaseless calling of your soul, deep down you will always be unfulfilled; even if you become a multi-millionaire with a string of houses, a yacht and a trophy wife or toy-boy.

Is it easy to free your soul so that it can fulfil its true purpose this lifetime? No! If it was easy, the whole world would be radiantly at peace by now. But the quest to free the soul is so worthwhile that I could not now imprison my soul again – not even for a billion pounds!

When you first awake, your soul is still rather weak, like a pale, flickering flame deep within you, while your personality-self's desires and moodiness still tend to exert a lot of influence over you. So at first, you will notice your soul only for a moment or two, and then this awareness will disappear and be replaced by fearful thoughts, desires and stormy emotions once again. Eventually however, your soul will grow much stronger and brighter, and then, all your self-centred, 'What about me?' thoughts will become more and more annoying to you, as you experience the indescribable joy of knowing your true-self.

Before you awake, you will always use your reason and logic to justify your anger, your attack thoughts, your fears and anxieties. A whoosh of anger shoots through you, and you will say to yourself, 'That man is just impossible to work with,' or 'My partner is impossible to live with.' But the more you awake, the more you will say to yourself, 'Whoops, there I go again getting angry over nothing. I had better go for a walk to calm down and notice the beauty of nature all around me.'

Your personality-self cannot stay in a totally peaceful, loving state of mind for long because basically it does not know what love is. Your personality-self has endless desires to fulfil. It even believes that a particularly strong desire for someone is 'true love'. But human desire for a sexual partner is not true, everlasting love. It is just a very powerful and entrancing type of egoic neediness.

However, your soul is not a 'me' self. Your soul knows true union and true love. So the more you awake and connect to your soul, the more you will simply long to share infinite love with the whole wide world. Moreover, as your soul awakes and grows stronger in the light, you will become so much more charismatic. You will become softer and much more graceful, but at the same time you will shine your inner light out into the world much more powerfully. At this point, you will become a safe haven to shelter and illuminate other souls who are still trapped in the darkness.

When your soul is awake, you will feel so much more at ease. Suddenly, in a moment of pure awakening, you will connect to your soul and realise 'Wow! This is the real me!' As you more and more tune into your soul, you will care less and less about being right, or about attaining worldly acclaim. Someone will try to take the credit for all your hard work, and you will not even think about getting annoyed with them. Someone will try and pick an argument with you, but you will just smile because you will genuinely experience no need to defend yourself. For example, someone will tell you the political party that you have supported all your life is a disaster for the country, and you will no longer feel compelled to leap to its defence.

As you awake to the truth, you will begin to live in a much more peaceful, less conflicted world. You will feel so much more at ease, and other people may even argue with you less. In fact, the whole world will seem to have been transformed in front of your very eyes. People all around you may still be getting so uptight about the latest political scandal, economic crisis, or environmental disaster, but you will notice that you are still at peace. Now can you see why we all need to awake and to connect to the infinite peace at the very core of our being before we can live in peace in this world?

Without Awakening We Cannot See Clearly

Genuinely kind, unselfish, understanding people are still a minority in our world, and so our whole world is still a mess. Most people are still out to get what they can for themselves and their families, regardless of the consequences for others. Moreover, even very kind individuals still suffer terribly in our world. When someone who has dedicated their lives to helping others gets cancer, we tend to say, 'Life is so unfair!' No. We simply do not understand how life actually works. Without awakening, individuals do not really see life clearly at all.

Basically, most of humankind is deluded. A close friend or a relative makes one remark about us that really upsets us, and suddenly they have become our enemy. How can this be? Does this make sense to you? It has always seemed insane to me, but before I awoke, I just could not explain it.

Until we are spiritually awake, we all tend to interpret the world through our subjective, pre-programmed beliefs and so we all see the world very differently. One person sees butter as a potential killer, whilst another is convinced it is good for them. One person sees Muslim radicals as brave heroes; the next condemns them as potential terrorists. No wonder we all feel so lonely! Not even our own partners or children can completely share our personal views and beliefs about life.

12

It is so difficult to relate to one another in any truly meaningful way because we are all seeing a very different world through the unique prism of our own mind. You can write a whole essay about the harsh things your parents said or did to you when you were little, and even now they often irritate you. But then you introduce your parents to your best friend, and she finds them delightful. Moreover, if you confront your mother with the terribly hurtful telling off she gave you when you were seven, she will tell you she absolutely does not remember doing any such thing.

Seeing How Crazy We Are

What to do? Well to begin with, we just need to understand that the key to changing our world is to change our own mind. If we simply go on looking outwards and blaming the world for all our suffering, absolutely nothing is going to change. So, we have to be brave, look within, and see just how crazy most of our thoughts are.

Until we awake, we are a bit like a paranoid schizophrenic who sees danger all around him, when in reality, no danger exists. The paranoid schizophrenic can even believe his own mother is an evil monster who wants to kill him. We can all see how crazy this is, and yet when we tell ourselves that our own loving mother is the most irritating or most uncaring person on the planet, we tend not to see the craziness of our own thinking.

Most people really do not want to see how insane and dark their egoic minds are, and so they will resist taking on an awakening practice such as meditation. They will insist they cannot meditate, when really they are just not ready to change their minds about themselves and the world. You need some real courage to begin to change your own mind from dwelling in fear and darkness to dwelling in love and light. But there is really no other totally effective and long-lasting way to improve our lives and the lives of others.

In the late 20th century, we began to witness a spiritual renaissance in the Western world and now genuine spiritual teachings, both ancient and modern, are widely available to us. However, a lot of spiritual seekers are not yet fully prepared to look at their own inner darkness and so they remain part-time seekers. They go on a weekend meditation workshop once in a while, and then they see themselves as spiritual, but they do not master any one genuine spiritual practice that always involves looking directly at our shadow side.

Most of my students are spiritual seekers who are looking for the real thing. They are highly intelligent and mature individuals who understand the limitations of the intellect and of pursuing worldly forms of happiness, and so they have begun to search for something that will give them the lasting peace and love that they long for. Many of my students eventually become strong and brave enough to look directly at their own inner fear and darkness, but even so, a number of individuals who sign up for my Ling Chi Healing Course, do not complete it. This may well be because they are just not yet ready to heal the deepest layers of their inner darkness.

Raising Our Consciousness

A lot of highly intelligent, well-educated Westerners are still trapped in their intellect, without realising the miraculous benefits of going beyond it and connecting to the awakening, healing light. Our intellect is great, but it has serious limitations. It cannot fill our whole being with a blissful sense of love and beauty, in the way that pure nature, great art or meditative practices can.

Most of us are now lost in our thoughts. We think constantly and believe that thinking can solve virtually all of our problems. We do not realise that when we are lost in thought, we are not fully alive because real life lies beyond all thought. Positive thinking is certainly better for us than fearful, negative thinking, but we need to raise our consciousness to a level beyond thought, before we can finally restore sanity back to our deluded minds.

If you learn to take time out from thinking on a regular basis, you will feel great, even if your personality-self finds non-thinking quite boring. Most people block out their awareness of non-dualistic reality with their constant fearful thinking about 'me'. But if we commit to learning how to rise above our thinking, we can eventually discover the bliss of a thought-free state of mind.

So let us conclude this brief introduction to Infinite Awakening by summing up the foundations of all genuine awakening paths: to raise your own consciousness out of the darkness of unawakened human existence, you will need to cultivate some skilful means, such as meditation and contemplation, some spiritual will-power, and some real mental toughness because no-one ever said that the awakening path is a walk in the park! However, my loving wish for you dear reader is that reading this book may give you some truly helpful ideas and practices to assist you on your way to the bliss of awakened living.

Meditation

*My soul is longing to break free and I am
determined to find out how to release it from
the darkness into the light.*

Sit quietly and comfortably with a straight spine and take
3 or 4 deep, conscious breaths to relax your body and mind.

Now see or imagine an exceptionally bright star above
your crown centre illuminating your whole being with this
higher light.

Stay in meditation for 15-20 minutes just bathing in this
higher light until you feel a sense of being totally supported
by a much higher power.

If at any point in your meditation you find that you
have become lost in your thoughts, gently let them go
and return to focussing on your breath and the light that
is surrounding and supporting you.

At the end of this meditation, give thanks for the higher
energy you have received and then choose a time and
a place to meditate in the light again tomorrow.

Chapter Two

Building Firm Foundations

Don't Be a Part-Time Spiritual Seeker

Some spiritual speakers, like Marianne Williamson, have star quality. They can change the atmosphere in a large hall and ignite a fire in the human heart. However, once they finish speaking, their audience tends to go back to their previous state of mind pretty quickly. Even though many of those in an inspired audience vow to themselves they will become more spiritual, or more awake, once they go home and return to their normal worldly lives, all their good intentions tend to fly out of the window.

I have also noticed that after leaving my retreats filled with love and light, participants usually experience what I call the 'Going Home Syndrome'. They tend to get irritated over minor matters and start believing once again in sickness, betrayal and abandonment. Why do we all do this over and over again, after we have enjoyed some time out from the constant conflict and anxiety of day to day human life?

Unfortunately, our negative default programming is so strong, and so deeply embedded in our psyche, it will take a heroic effort to overcome it. Basically, to transcend a very powerful pattern of sinking down into fear and depression, you have to transform yourself so that you no longer think like a normal human being. Without this ultimate goal, you are just a part-time spiritual seeker, a weekend 'Spiritual Warrior'.

Once in a blue moon spiritual experiences are not enough. To really reap the benefits of your spiritual practice, you need to attain higher states of consciousness on a very regular basis. Higher beings will assist you every step of the way on your awakening journey, but they will never push you forwards against your will. You will have to walk every step of the way under your own steam.

Pursuing a spiritual path like a hobby just does not work. You need to plug into the light — a commonly used symbol for a very high, pure energy filled with higher wisdom and guidance — every day of your life, not just twice a year at a Mind Body Spirit festival, or once a month on some kind of spiritual course. You need to keep connecting to the light with all your heart and soul on a daily basis, if you are to stand any chance of transforming and then transcending your fearful, disconnected egoic-self.

In this chapter, I will outline a whole set of powerful spiritual tools you can use on a daily basis. Not many spiritual teachers cover so many different disciplines, including energy work. But I have witnessed over and over again that what I am teaching really works — as long as my students put my suggestions into practice in their daily lives on a *very* regular basis.

Building Your Spiritual Strength

Cultivating true spiritual strength is so important! At times on their miraculous journey home, awakening individuals tend to experience even more anxiety than other people, as the light illuminates all of their previously hidden fear and darkness. Fear will accompany you on your spiritual journey for a very long time, so you might as well make friends with it. To do this, you will need to build up your inner strength and courage. Then, and only then, can you make a heroic effort to transcend fear each and every time it threatens to overwhelm you.

Iconic world heroes, such as Nelson Mandela and the Dalai Lama, have become universal role models by demonstrating a tremendous inner strength combined with true compassion. Sadly, most human beings have not yet cultivated these two essential qualities. When most people are served just one bad meal by a grumpy waiter, all of their loving kindness towards others simply flies out of the window.

We are all so petty! What on earth is going on? Basically, we have not yet cultivated enough spiritual will to override the tantrums thrown by our ego. Even in an exceptionally peaceful and beautiful environment, such as a 5* hotel on a tropical island, one meal that we do not enjoy can send us into a temper tantrum.

When we first step onto our awakening path, we may have some idea about what we want to gain from listening to spiritual teachers or reading spiritual texts, but we simply do not have the capacity to hold the light for any length of time. So our egoic desires and aversions continue to disrupt our inner peace – big time. We therefore need to strengthen and reinforce our spiritual will on a daily basis, because our subconscious default programme is so dark and fearful that it creates mayhem in our own life and in the lives of all our loved ones.

Advanced Spiritual Teachings Can Be Misinterpreted

One of the highest universal spiritual truths is that this whole physical existence is just an illusion or a fleeting dream. But because our physical existence is now the only one we know, we cling to it for dear life and then it can certainly feel very real to us.

You may have heard the spiritual teaching that your physical body does not really exist. It is relatively easy for seekers to misunderstand this advanced spiritual truth, and then to tell themselves that they therefore do not have to try to achieve anything in this illusionary world. Some seekers may even conclude that they can do whatever they like in this world without any lasting consequences, because it is all just a dream.

Occasionally, a rather insensitive spiritual practitioner may even tell someone suffering from cancer that their sickness is just an illusion in their mind. This is extremely unhelpful and unkind. The causes of a nasty disease like cancer are so complex! Dismissing a friend's cancer as just an illusion is a total misinterpretation of a very deep and abstruse spiritual teaching.

If you have ever told yourself your body does not matter that much because it is not ultimately real, or that money is all make-believe, so why bother managing it carefully, you are misinterpreting some profound spiritual teachings. I always tell my students that whilst we have a physical body, we need to do our very best to look after it. If you have a mortgage, you really do have to keep paying it off. If you have a family, you should do your very best to be kind, loving and forgiving to your family members at all times.

I really do not agree with anyone who says 'I don't have to do anything to make this world a better place because it is all just an illusion.' I believe we all need to keep making choices that support life. For example, whilst you have a physical body, you should choose a healthy diet rich in fresh, natural ingredients.

But a healthy diet alone is not enough to support a radiant life. We also need to open our hearts to love. We need to do this on a daily basis so that we can become fully awake and alive, and then support others to be fully alive too. We also need to study and practise spiritual teachings that resonate deeply with our heart's longing to return home to love.

Unfortunately, studying and practising spiritual teachings in the 21st century is not always straightforward. To begin with, if you are serious about longing to awake, you need to develop some discerning wisdom so that you can find a genuine awakening path, rather than getting caught up in what we might call 'pseudo-spiritual' pursuits. One magazine article I came across recently was entitled 'Energise Your Chakras with Healing Cupcakes'. There is certainly nothing wrong with baking 'healing' cupcakes if it appeals to you. It has just got nothing to do with awakening and deep spiritual truths.

If you are serious about your path, you need to study a range of spiritual teachings until you develop real insight into the difference between the miraculous truth about life and all fearful illusions. You also need to aim to accumulate some direct spiritual experiences that will provide you with those 'Ah ha' moments during which you suddenly get a previously elusive truth. Ironically, the more you study genuine spiritual teachings, the more you will realise that your intellectual mind just does not understand the truth, and so you will begin to let go of many, if not all, of your intellectual beliefs about what is spiritual and what is not.

If enlightenment was as easy as some New Age books suggest, everyone would be enlightened by now. To make real progress on any awakening path, you actually have to become quite obsessive about searching for the truth. When I was first seeking, I would stay up all night reading an inspiring spiritual text, before having to go to work early the next morning.

But please understand that studying awakening is not the same as practising awakening. Some people have read many excellent spiritual books, but they have not put what they read into practice in their lives. So many people have read Eckhart Tolle's *The Power of Now*, for example, but how many people actually practise bringing their mind back over and over again to the present moment, so that they can access 'The Power of Now' for themselves? Similarly, quite a few people in our society are now familiar with some modern Buddhist texts, and may even have read a bit of *A Course in Miracles*, but far, far fewer individuals are putting the spiritual principles outlined in these texts into practice on a regular basis.

Putting Spiritual Principles into Practice

There are now so many different awakening paths for us to choose from. But to make any real progress, you need to commit to one spiritual system, such as one type of Buddhism or *A Course in Miracles*, and then put its principles into practice in your daily life, without deviating or prevaricating, otherwise your egoic fear and anger will continue to take you over. Living your life according to key spiritual principles, such as forgiveness or compassion, does not mean that you will never be moody or incensed. But you will at least be building up your spiritual muscles, as you try to replace your grievances with miracles, (*A Course in Miracles*) or to cultivate compassion for your enemies. (Buddhism)

Putting spiritual principles into practice in your own life is certainly challenging, but also incredibly rewarding once you taste the miraculous fruits of serious spiritual endeavour.

At first, if you try to practise the spiritual virtue of generosity, for example, you may notice how rarely you give generously to others without expecting some kind of personal return on your investment. For some time, if you practise generosity seriously, you will actually notice your self-centredness more, not less. Similarly, if you start to practise the virtue of patience or forbearance, you may well seem to become more rather than less impatient, as your awareness of your tendency to be easily irritated by life's little hold-ups gets stronger and stronger.

22

Please don't despair! Becoming aware of just how much we tend to sabotage any chance we have of lasting peace and joy is one of the great benefits of all genuine spiritual practices.

Thankfully, following spiritual principles such as cultivating generosity and patience, and forgiving our 'enemies', can eventually re-programme our minds away from fear and neurotic self-centredness and toward compassion for all sentient beings including, of course, ourselves.

The Core Spiritual Practice of Meditation

When you are not in a meditative state, you are more or less dreaming your life away. You think negative, fearful thoughts quite a lot of the time, even in your sleep, and your life has no lasting peace or joy in it. You may be sitting in a beautiful park eating a delicious picnic lunch with your loved ones, and yet you still feel anxious, annoyed or depressed to some degree or other.

A few years ago, the front page of Time Magazine stated that millions of stressed-out Americans were taking up meditation. I predict that eventually, those Westerners who don't meditate will be in the minority because collective consciousness is changing, and more and more individuals are waking up to the amazing benefits of a regular meditation practice. As they do so, this classic spiritual skill will become much easier to master and then everyone will be clamouring to learn it.

Scientists have now observed that long term meditators can reverse the ageing process in their cells, and can also produce 'happy' hormones in much greater amounts than non-meditators. Some researchers are also beginning to document the problem-solving potential of mindfulness meditation. So I predict that in maybe 20-30 years' time, at least some innovative company executives will be saying, 'We have a problem. Let's meditate on it.'

However, we each need to find some peace or pleasure in meditation, or we will have no motivation to keep up our practice. So, one of my key goals, when I lead my students in Infinite Meditation, is to assist them in discovering for themselves the incredible feeling of inner peace, joy and love that genuine meditation can give us.

The extreme state of well-being that experienced meditators can reach is unmistakable and incredibly desirable. Once your chattering mind is still, your core-being can simply bask in love and light. But not so many meditators can sustain this level of awakening because as soon as they start to think once again, they lose themselves once more in regrets about the past or fantasies about the future.

Building Your Practice Step by Step

Spiritual practices are incremental. Each and every time you meditate, for example, the effects of your practice increase and the fruits of your meditations grow sweeter and juicier. You have to experience a deep meditative state of mind thousands of times, until you are completely familiar and at ease with the energy of pure love and light. Only then, will you begin to grow in the light like a beautiful sunflower. So please, keep taking time out from your daily life to practise the supreme art of meditation, until infinite love and light fully permeate your individual consciousness.

Sometimes, experienced meditators can reach a plateau at which they feel really great, and they may want to hang out there for some time. But if you are determined to achieve complete self-liberation, even when you reach the higher stages of the path, you can request a higher power to push you onwards and upwards so that you can continue to grow, even if the next stretch of your path is extremely steep and challenging.

Whenever you reach another plateau on your climb up the spiritual mountain, you can rest for a while from the challenges of the ascent. Each time you grow spiritually, you will inevitably experience some growing pains. Then, you will reach another plateau and feel comfortable again for a while. At the higher levels of the path, the views are amazing. Life will seem so beautiful and you will experience true love and goodness everywhere. Everything in the universe will seem to come together to support your life and your highest dreams.

When you finally stand on the spiritual mountain top, you will experience no suffering and no struggle. At this level of consciousness, your soul is definitely safe, and you will certainly experience being in some kind of heavenly realm of existence after your body dies. But you can still choose to go for yet another level of awakening and healing that is waiting for you 'beyond the mountaintop'.

Whenever we consciously choose to go for another level of awakening and healing, life can feel quite uncomfortable for a while as we are divinely shaken out of our latest comfort zone.

At the highest levels of awakening, some practitioners may even experience a 'dark night of the soul' during which they may plunge into a state of existential fear or despair for quite some time, as they clear some very deep, collective, egoic paranoia out of their consciousness. But of course, as you climb higher and higher on your unique spiritual path, the views become more and more spectacular, and so even going through a 'dark night of the soul' – a core aspect of the deepest layer of our self-healing – is so worth it!

Energy Work

Raising our consciousness higher and higher has amazing benefits, but it is not enough to 'save the world'. Some individuals can connect to the light within their minds and hearts, but their physical bodies can still be frail. Ideally, if you want to go out and help the world in some way or another, you will cultivate a strong vibrant body, as well as an illuminated mind and heart. Unless we really strengthen our physical bodies, the higher spiritual light is just too pure and powerful for us to embody it for any length of time.

If someone who holds a lot of light in their heart and mind has a very frail body, those who resonate with their energy may still be able to tune into that light when they are in their presence. However, those who do not know how to tune in like this cannot benefit from the presence of a physically frail enlightened master, whereas, someone who is physically strong and vibrant, for example Barack Obama before he was elected President of the US, has a charisma and presence that ordinary people can feel, and so they can influence very large numbers of people.

Most spiritual paths do not include energy work, but in my experience, energy work, such as tai chi or chi kung, can really assist us to create a truly happy and fulfilling life for ourselves. Moreover cultivating strong, radiant inner energy can be even more important for those of us who want to be of real service to humanity. To be successful in any endeavour in this world, including any kind of spiritual work, we need to cultivate strong, balanced energy or chi.

To feel totally alive, you need to be filled with radiant inner energy. Cultivating chi can also help you to feel safe and to stay safe in this world. You can pack chi into your whole body to become strong and healthy. You need a very strong, healthy body to be an effective spiritual practitioner in this world. Try illuminating yourself with the light when you have flu, and you will see what I mean.

You also need to cultivate strong chi to sustain 'Shen' (Spirit) so that you will be able to focus one-pointedly on your spiritual practice. Shen is related to your third eye, and when your third eye is open, you will have much more focus during your meditations. Your thinking mind alone will not give you this essential focus. You need vibrant energy and open higher energy centres to connect to the light and then to embody that light. Nothing in this world, let alone enlightenment, can be accomplished without focus, and to sustain focus, we need a lot of internal energy.

Managing Your Energy

To stay strong and focussed on the path, you also need to know how to manage your energy levels so that you never get too energetically high or too low. You need to know, for example, how to raise your energy when you are feeling low and how to lower your energy, if you go too high and start to feel spacey or ungrounded.

If your energy soars too high in an unmanageable way, you may even go manic or slightly mad. On the other hand, if your energy plunges down too low, you may find that you are depressed, or extremely lethargic. So you should always aim to attain a sense of being filled with vibrant energy, but in a relaxed and calm way.

Most people do not know how to protect and enliven themselves with radiant chi. But I show my students how to protect themselves energetically, by cultivating radiant chi through their daily practice of The Infinite Arts. We can really empower ourselves with a radiant inner energy that I call 'chi abundance'. Once we know how to cultivate chi, we can then hold it throughout our whole system, and it will then protect us against low energy thoughts and feelings, such as anger, fear and jealousy.

If you keep topping yourself up with radiant inner energy, whilst simultaneously focussing your mind on love rather than fear, you will suffer far less, and thus inflict far less suffering on others. You will become a radiant, benign and beautiful human being.

Practise becoming vibrant on a daily basis, through some kind of holistic exercise such as yoga, tai chi or chi kung, and you can still be vibrant even in so called extreme old age. I refuse to believe in collective ideas about ageing. I am determined to be strong and radiantly healthy in my 80s. For me, the secret to positive ageing is to diligently keep cultivating 'chi abundance'. If you cultivate chi abundance and sunshine energy whilst you are still relatively strong and healthy, you should never grow frail and so you can age with real dignity and joy.

Planting Good Karmic Seeds

Occasionally, I have witnessed a student who practices energy work and meditation very diligently, but who does not seem to be reaping any fruits from their intense efforts. What is going wrong? Well my intuition tells me that some individuals who train with me have not yet built up enough good karma to reap the benefits of any genuine spiritual practices.

The Western world does not yet really understand the Eastern concept of karma. There is no scientific evidence about past karma and so this idea is not in the Western zeitgeist yet. But the more you raise your consciousness, the more you should be able to see limitations still imposed on your life by your past karma.

A lot of New Age books now talk vaguely about karma, without telling us how to transcend our own negative karma. But if you have any negative past karma – and basically all human beings do – it now has to be released so that your soul can expand further. Sometimes, you may just have to endure a karmic relationship, illness, or money problem for quite some time before that particular karma is released.

But you can always pray for divine assistance to transcend your karma. For example, in a deep meditation, you can utilise the power of your expanded awareness to connect to divine streams of energy such as Kuan Yin or Mother Mary. These divine mothers of love and compassion will always respond to any genuine calls for help. Moreover, the more you expand your consciousness, the more the divine light will stream through you, and this divine light and love can definitely assist you to transform your karma.

If you are not happy most of the time, maybe you have not yet planted enough happiness seeds in your mind or perhaps you have not yet sown enough happiness seeds in the world? When was the last time you focussed on making someone else really happy with no ulterior motive? I think that Robert Holden, who is director of 'The Happiness Project', must be an exceptionally happy guy because he has worked tirelessly to show other people how to be happier.

Do you realise that you are now sitting on all of your past karma; both positive and negative? You cannot even begin to awake, until you clear some negative karma from your system. Please do not take this personally. As evolving souls, we have all been around for thousands of years. We have all killed and been killed. This has nothing to do with being a good or bad person. I repeat: having some negative past karma to clear does not make you a bad person in any way whatsoever! It is just how life is: a never ending wheel of karma that creates our future, until we transcend all of it.

Your current life is the fruit of the seeds you have planted and then cultivated in the past. So how are you doing these days? How much do you like the life you are living now? How much do you love it? If your life is not yet fantastic, you may need to cultivate some more love or forgiveness seeds that will grow into wonderfully fruitful happiness plants.

This is 'practical spirituality'. You meditate first to set your intention for the day, week, month or even year ahead, and then you cultivate good karmic seeds by the selfless actions you perform in your daily life. For example, you can meditate on loving kindness and really feel this divine quality in your mind and heart, and then devote at least part of your day to performing small acts of loving kindness for others.

If you practise like this day in and day out, your karmic fruits should be sweet and full of sunshine energy. A beautiful life is never just handed to us on a plate. Many people's lives are basically miserable because they have no idea how to create a wonderful life for themselves. They do not realise that whenever we give selflessly to others, we are planting healthy seeds for a truly joyful future for ourselves.

Performing selfless acts of kindness and serving others with no thought of personal reward can really help you to transcend the core selfishness of the egoic 'me' and the more or less constant egoic thought, 'What about me?' Your meditation practice, certainly in the first few years of the path, is all about 'you'. But performing selfless service, even on a very small scale, can really assist you to transcend the self-centredness of the ego, until you finally develop the mentality of a saint or bodhisattva.

The Buddhist Mahayana path of selfless action is basically training saints or bodhisattvas as they are called in the Buddhist tradition. When advanced Buddhist practitioners commit themselves to the Bodhisattva path, they make others' enlightenment as important, if not more important, than their own. Similarly, *A Course in Miracles* talks about taking your brother and sister with you when you enter heaven, rather than trying to get there on your own.

To start with, you will probably notice some resentment rising up as you try to serve others selflessly. 'Me' is a very short word, but it is so powerful! Trying to suppress this self-centred me through self-denial rarely works. Think of those Catholic priests who tried to suppress their sexual desires and failed disastrously. But transcending 'me' through selfless service definitely works in the long run, and you can even 'fake it until you make it'. You can simply go on performing a selfless action even whilst your ego is screaming, 'What about me? This is so unfair!'

Embodying the Teachings

More and more individuals may now be following some kind of spiritual path, but we do not yet have many Jesus Christs or Buddhas walking on earth today.

Embodying genuine spiritual teachings takes decades of extremely dedicated and skilled practice. Just cultivating mindfulness, for example, by learning to keep our mind focussed on the present moment, can take years of serious application.

Studying and practising spiritual teachings is at the core of all spiritual apprenticeships. Embodying the teachings is mastership. This is your ultimate goal. But please do not be too hard on yourself when you find yourself slipping back from time to time into egoic fear, or attack. The personality-self is very sticky and sneaky and it will not disappear without first putting up a very good fight. But every time you notice that you are once again at the mercy of the egoic thought system, just remind yourself that you have been given another wonderful invitation to heal and awake further. No big deal!

Once you have mastered your own awakening path, you will naturally want to support humanity in some way or another. Please be assured that in this advanced stage of your spiritual journey, heaven will bow down to assist you. You are like the 'Hero' in Jo Campbell's *The Hero's Journey* who goes on an incredibly challenging adventure in order to strengthen and test himself and to discover the wonderful truth about life, and who then returns home to become a shining example for others to follow.

Once you are ready to spread the light, all the angels in heaven will vow to assist you. You will also miraculously meet all the right people down here on earth who will support you in your light-work. You will naturally attract into your radiant presence all those individuals who have been waiting for you to embody the light so that you can extend it to them and awaken them in their turn.

The awakening path is always a path into the complete unknown, which is one reason why all are called to tread the path, but few choose to answer the call. It takes a brave and trusting individual to keep going down a particular path for years on end, without having a clue where they are going. Everyone I have asked to 'spread the light' with me has gone through a lot of fear and self-doubt, and not everyone has answered the call, but some have stuck with me through thick and thin, and together we have created something truly beautiful in this world.

Please note that you cannot just leap from being a spiritual student to being an enlightened spiritual teacher or healer. It takes so much training to become a genuine light-worker. Moreover, if you take a vow to selflessly serve your brothers and sisters by extending love and light to them, you really have to mean it.

St. Francis of Assisi really meant it when he prayed, 'Lord, make me an instrument of your peace.' Heartfelt prayers such as this are extremely powerful, but even if your intention to help others is exceptionally strong and sincere, you will probably still have to go through a long and arduous training to become an effective light-worker.

'As God is my witness, I vow to transcend all of my limitations until I become a perfect channel for God's love, light and peace.' If you say this with real conviction, it is an incredibly powerful prayer. If you *really* mean it, you can certainly transform all of your personal weaknesses into spiritual strengths, and all of your self-centredness into selflessness. However, all this does take time and effort. You will have to keep purifying and strengthening yourself step by step for many years, until your personality-self has been transmuted from gross metal into spiritual gold.

I had to learn so much before I could even begin to do the work that I am now doing. I had to train myself up in all sorts of ways. Twenty year ago, I certainly could not have done what I do today.

Please do not waste any more precious time. Just keep following a straight and narrow spiritual path, until you fully embody the light and thus become a shining star for other suffering souls to follow. Do you think that only Jesus Christ could perform miracles? Please think again. Once you are on a genuine awakening path, you are being trained to become a miracle worker, and nothing else in this world could ever fulfil you as much as this soul calling.

So my sincere prayer for you is that you find your unique awakening path and then keep going along it, come what may. Your partner divorces you: keep going. You fall madly in love with a new partner: keep practising. You get really sick: keep meditating. You go on a luxury world cruise: get up early every morning to do your tai chi or yoga on the upper deck. Don't let anything stand in your way, or you will seriously regret it. Keep moving forwards step by step on your unique path, until you reach the very top of the spiritual mountain. But in the meantime, please make sure that you fully enjoy all the fabulous views along the way.

Meditation

My actions today are creating either my future suffering or my future happiness.

Sit quietly in a meditative position, see or imagine a bright star above your crown centre and breathe its illuminating light into every cell of your being.

Calm your thinking mind for a while by letting your thoughts come and go without focussing on them.

Now ask the light or your own spiritual guide: 'How good is my karma in relation to my health, my finances and my relationships?'

Sit meditatively for 15-20 minutes allowing the higher light to answer your question.

At the end of this meditation intuitively write down a number from one (poor) to ten (excellent) to represent your health karma/money karma/ relationship karma.

Finally ask: 'What small action could I perform today, so that I begin to plant some fruitful karmic seeds for my future. For example, if you have money problems, think of a small act of generosity that you could perform for someone later in the day.

Once you have thought of this action, tell yourself, 'As the Light is my witness, I will do this today without fail'. Then just rest in the light for a while longer before continuing with your day.

Chapter Three

Lower Levels of Consciousness

Lower Levels of Consciousness

Life Supporting Consciousness	200 +
- -	
Pride	175
Anger/Hatred	150
Desire	125
Fear/Anxiety	100
Grief/Sorrow/Regret	75
Apathy/Despair	50
Guilt	30
Shame	20

Based on Dr. David R. Hawkins Map of Consciousness in 'Power v. Force' (2004)

If you are determined to transcend human pain and suffering for your own sake and the sake of others, you will need to keep raising your energy and your consciousness, until you are living in complete harmony with yourself and the world around you.

Typically, we live our whole lives in conflict with ourselves and others. Why? Because our consciousness is trapped in the low energy of negative human emotions, such as anger, fear, guilt and shame. At the start of our awakening/healing journey, we really have to make an effort to understand these low emotions, and then we have to practise rising above them.

Emotional moodiness is not at all easy to transcend because our stormy emotions always override our logic and reason. When we are fearful or angry, we tend to tell ourselves stories to justify our moodiness, and then we invest a lot of energy in our version of events, until it becomes completely real to us. But our interpretations of the world are not based on reality. They are like fairy stories in which we play the role of innocent victim and others the role of wicked step-mother or Big Bad Wolf.

To date, very few human beings have realised that they create their own reality through the stories they tell themselves and the emotions that accompany these stories. For example, every time you tell yourself that you hate someone, or that someone is your 'enemy', you are creating a horrible reality for yourself.

We all have an emotional 'pain body' that Eckhart Tolle has described as *a negative energy field that occupies your body and mind.* Every time we indulge in 'poor me' thoughts or 'I hate' stories, this pain body grows bigger. For example, a belief such as 'I hate my father,' will create real conflict in our mind and heart. However, nearly all of us hold some negative beliefs like this, and so we all have some internal conflict that causes us stress and pain. Sadly, until we begin to awake, we have no idea that we have a choice about which beliefs and feelings we allow into our mind and heart.

Most adults are emotionally crippled to some degree or other because they lack basic information on how to handle all their feelings, particularly the really painful, imprisoning feelings of jealousy, rage, guilt or shame. As yet, no one teaches young people how to cope with all of this, which, in my opinion, is a tragedy for the whole human race.

My students and clients often ask me, 'What should I do?' 'Should I change my job?' 'Should I leave my partner?' I always say to them, 'Don't rush into any action. First and foremost, quieten your mind and calm your emotions. Make sure you are at peace before you make any irreversible decision. Never act when you are full of egoic pride, anger, fear or guilt, or you will inevitably make a mess'.

Most people are 'human doings' rather than human beings. We think that in order to be happier, we need to take some kind of action, but this is often a big mistake. Unless we can rise above egoic pride, fear, anger, hatred and guilt to find inner peace and harmony, whatever actions we take will not bring us the lasting peace and fulfilment we are seeking.

Of course, we may gain some temporary relief from our emotional pain by running away from a difficult situation or indulging in a soothing activity of some kind. But if we do not commit to healing the underlying painful beliefs that lower our energetic vibration and attract painful situations into our lives, we will soon find another soul-destroying job or a new abusive partner coming our way.

The key to creating a more peaceful and fulfilling life for ourselves is to raise our consciousness above the low levels of anger, fear, shame and guilt into the much higher levels of love and light. Day in and day out, we have to keep practising raising our consciousness so that we can rise above our emotional moodiness and start to dream a happy dream.

Most people are leading an unconscious existence and so they will evolve very slowly, if at all. However, on all of our Infinite Arts courses, we assist students to raise their energetic vibration through a very regular practise of Infinite Tai Chi, Infinite Chi Kung and Infinite Meditation, so that they can expand their consciousness and eventually know, rather than guess, what they should do with their lives. I also explain to my students how to recognise when they are trapped in negative emotions, so they at least have a choice about whether to stay trapped or to do their very best to free themselves.

Understanding Negative Human Emotions

All human emotions are just 'energy in motion'. Some emotions, such as love and joy, have high energy, and some, such as fear and guilt, have low energy. But if we simply open our mind, heart and body, and allow all emotions to flow through us unimpeded, none of them will do us any lasting harm. No feeling or emotion is your enemy, unless you make it so. You can befriend all of your emotions; even those that make you feel extremely uncomfortable, by gently holding them in open, higher awareness, and then releasing them into the ether.

But whenever we tense up against a particular emotion such as fear or jealousy, we block its natural flow through our system, and so its energy can get stuck deep inside us. The stored dark energy of suppressed emotions can then cause us all sorts of problems and may even make us physically ill. Alternatively, if we try to run away from uncomfortable emotions by projecting them outwards onto others, we can end up doing real harm to other living creatures.

The bottom line is that fear, which is a core element of compound negative emotions such as jealousy and guilt, is an enduring problem in our world because we just do not know how to handle it. However, once we are brave and determined enough to sit and face our deepest fears, we can begin to flow serenely through life, rather than drowning in endless waves of fear and anger.

One way in which our intellectual minds can grasp the danger of not rising above all of our negative emotions is to see their position on a calibration chart. According to Dr David R Hawkins who created a 'Map of Cconsciousness', based on the level at which certain emotions vibrate energetically, anything that calibrates below 200 does not support life, whereas anything that calibrates above 200 is life-supporting.

Pride (175)

According to Dr David R. Hawkins, egoic pride calibrates at 175, which is just below the level of energetic vibration that actually supports life.

Most human beings feel vulnerable in this world, but then we all try to cover up our deep sense of vulnerability and unworthiness with egoic pride. Please don't fall for this egoic trick. Egoic pride is always a weakness rather than a true strength. Moreover, whenever our egoic pride is hurt, we can very easily slip into feeling vengeful.

Egoic pride is very easily bruised, and when our pride is hurt, we will attack others to defend ourselves, and probably end up feeling even more unworthy, guilty or fearful. Pride can feel much more comfortable than a sense of unworthiness, but we all tend to flip between these two habitual egoic states. Whenever our pride is hurt, anger tends to be close at hand – 'You treat me like shit. Why the hell are you doing this to me?'

Pride is built into our human existence. Even very sincere spiritual teachers and healers can fall into the trap of egoic pride.

For example, they may start to feel superior to 'ordinary' human beings because they believe they can 'zap' others with the light, perform miraculous healings, or attract a large following of devotees. But spiritual pride can very easily lead to a fall, and so all spiritual practitioners have to guard carefully against falling into its trap.

Empowerment of any kind can turn nasty. Just think of Hitler. He was clearly a charismatic leader, but his own unhealed inner darkness, combined with his extraordinary power over a whole nation, unleashed a terrible holocaust onto the world. But Hitler was by no means unique. We all have a strong egoic tendency to misuse worldly power once we gain it. Bosses have a tendency to bully their subordinates, and teachers can sometimes humiliate their students.

Egoic pride combined with worldly power can be so destructive, but egoic pride can also be a dangerous trap on our inward spiritual journey. One way in which the ego may try to block your awakening is by hijacking all of your spiritual experiences. Your ego just loves to proclaim, 'I am now such a spiritual person!'

This is arrogant nonsense, but if you buy into it, you may delay your true spiritual advancement for a long, long time.

The only way to avoid the trap of egoic pride is to get to know how the ego really works in intimate detail. We then need to keep cultivating compassion and genuine humility to counterbalance our inbuilt tendency to become puffed up with our own 'special' spiritual experiences and achievements.

When you are fully awake, you will see how totally equal we all are in essence, and at that moment your egoic pride will naturally dissolve. True humility comes with identifying with your divinity and knowing that we are all divine in nature.

In ultimate reality, everyone and everything is equally glorious and perfect beyond your wildest dreams. When you truly see this for yourself, you will respect all of life and nurture it with unconditional love, rather than indulging in any thoughts of egoic, or even spiritual, superiority over others.

Anger/Hatred (150)

The energy of anger is high enough to make us *feel* alive, but not high enough to support our life in the long run.

In this world, anger can seem powerful because angry people can often bully or intimidate others into doing what they want them to do. But this type of power is superficial and temporary. It in no way matches the true power of spiritual radiance and defencelessness.

Anger combined with aggressiveness can certainly create some kind of control over others that seems to work, as others reluctantly submit to an aggressive attack. However, from a spiritual perspective, aggression is always self-defeating because it is simply self-attack projected outwards. Fortunately, as our consciousness rises and we connect to a higher dimension of life, we will naturally tend to become far less angry and aggressive. Eventually, even mildly aggressive thoughts, such as irritation with a selfish road user, will cause us pain. It can be shocking to see just how much anger and hatred we all hold in our system, but I assure you that seeing this is the first, crucial step to rising above it.

We all like to believe we love other people, particularly those closest to us, but the uncomfortable truth is that we are usually trying to get something from those whom we claim to love. Then, when we believe they are refusing to give us what we want, we get angry with them or even hate them for it. This uncomfortable truth explains why human love can so easily turn to hate.

One moment you adore your partner, and the next, when they tell you they are leaving or having an affair, you really hate them. How can this be true love? True love is always totally unconditional and non-judgemental. True love is complete in and of itself and needs absolutely nothing from anyone. But the ego just cannot love like this. Only your higher-self can love someone unconditionally. Only your higher-self can love someone without simultaneously attacking them.

When I was a young man and my girlfriend left me for another guy, I resented him so much that I even imagined punching him. It is very fortunate that we are all so afraid of being caught and punished for breaking the law, otherwise a lot more of us might act out our thoughts of hatred towards our 'enemies' in aggressive ways. Even so called civilised individuals can indulge in violent thoughts, such as 'I wish you would just drop dead.'

Very angry thoughts such as these can give us a temporary energetic buzz, but in the long run, they simply increase our sense of unworthiness and deep guilt. Then, if we keep refusing to face own our self-hatred, we will find we just have to project it out onto others and say to ourselves, 'They are the guilty ones. They deserve to be punished, not me'.

Until we awake, we all project our anger and self-hatred outwards onto others and blame them for our own pain and suffering. Some individuals with very low levels of consciousness may rape and torture others in order to feel better about themselves. A terrorist may even attempt to blow many people into smithereens in an unconscious attempt to ease their own deep inner pain.

Of course, this sounds insane to us, but we actually do the same thing albeit in a much less violent way. We think gossiping negatively about someone, or attacking them angrily with sarcastic words, will ease our own pain, but this too is insane. However, please don't take this statement too personally. Our collective human psyche is still very dark and twisted and even exceptionally good, kind people still find themselves attacking others; if only with their angry, judgemental thoughts.

Fear (100)

Fear is even lower than anger on Dr David R. Hawkin's Map of Consciousness. The energy of fear is cold and weak, and so whenever we are fearful, we weaken our whole system. Unfortunately, all human beings are intrinsically fearful from the day we are born.

We are all born in fear, and then as we grow and learn to think, our thinking is always tinted with fear or anxiety. The whole collective human mindset is so fearful; we are all a little bit paranoid. Before we experience a spiritual awakening, we are all mildly anxious at best and terrified at worst. A physically strong and aggressive person may well think they are not fearful, but basically they are just trying to project their own fear outwards by making others frightened. A torturer, for example, may well feel no fear whilst he is torturing his victim, but in the long run, he cannot escape his own inner fear and darkness.

When we are living in fear and lack, we can all be aggressive, as we try to grab what we think we lack from others. When we live in poverty consciousness for example, we tend to assume, not always consciously, that someone has stolen our rightful inheritance from us and we now have a right to try and grab it back. In recent years, many poor people struggling with rising debt have convinced themselves that greedy bankers are the ones responsible for their plight. Similarly, whole countries can assume they have a right to attack their enemies because they believe these enemies threaten their way of life.

Countries now spend ridiculous amounts on national security and defence. For example, the American defence budget is now over 600 billion dollars a year! Fearful individuals also spend a lot of money to protect themselves from all kinds of external attacks. Unfortunately, none of this massive spending on defence and security really works because fear and conflict are inevitable in a world ruled by a collective, paranoid, egoic thought system.

So whenever I teach Infinite Tai Chi, one of my primary goals is to assist my students to feel safe, or at least safer. When we feel safe and secure, we will be far less likely to attack. When we feel empowered by the light, our paranoia will begin to fade. Truly empowered individuals tend to feel safe enough to be exceptionally kind and generous, whereas disempowered people tend to be moody, volatile and even downright dangerous.

Fear is a primary human emotion. We are all afraid of something. What frightens you? Please make a list of all your main fears, so that you can begin to see them clearly. Fear is a really big, troublesome issue for all human beings, and so we need to devote a lot of time and attention to healing our major fears before they overwhelm us.

What external symbols have you created to represent your inner fears? Are you afraid of spiders, snakes, heights or confined spaces? We all tend to project our fear outwards like this. So we all tend to have a list of external objects that really seem to frighten us. Extreme fear can actually paralyse you, and even in its less extreme forms, fear leaves you loveless, because true love and fear can never coexist. So if you want to return home to love, you have to conquer all your fears one by one.

Grief (75)

Grief is a complex, low energy emotion with elements of sadness, fear and even anger in it. No wonder that grief-stricken individuals can find it almost impossible to function normally in our society, when all they have the energy to do is to curl up in a ball and cry.

All human beings will experience some grief in their life. It just seems to be inbuilt in our basic make-up. Some individuals seem to be constantly grieving, and every time you meet them, you can sense this. For others, the emotion of grief can fade from their consciousness quite quickly, so you may have to really search your mind to recall your experiences of the feeling of grief.

Grief and longing at the loss of a loved one, whether through death or the break-up of a relationship, are at heart the same feeling as the deep longing and loss we all feel because of our apparent separation from God. Transcending deep grief is not at all easy to do and can sometimes take a very long time. So you need to cultivate great love and compassion for yourself, as you gently release all of your grief and thoughts of loss into the light. You also need to be brave 'enough to face the pain stored in your broken heart so that you can finally mend it. As well as being exceptionally kind to yourself when you are grieving, please also cultivate infinite patience with grieving loved ones. Never tell anyone, for example, that it is time that they got over their loss and moved on with their life. Who are we to judge how long someone else should grieve for? Just support a grieving friend or relative with your unconditional love, compassion and inner strength and allow them the right to grieve for as long as they choose to do so.

Depression/Apathy (50)

Depression is associated with extremely low energy. So if you allow yourself to sink down into a depressed state, it can be almost impossible to pull yourself out of it.

Depression is linked to extreme disappointment with life. But disappointment is something we all feel at some point in our lives. Unconsciously, until we are fully healed and awake, we set others up to disappoint us, especially our parents and our intimate partners. For example, we may hold a belief in abandonment deep in our subconscious mind, and then we wonder why others act in ways that simply confirm our past programming.

We believe that others can betray us, and then we say to ourselves, 'I just do not trust men/women anymore', or 'What is the point in even trying to find a loving relationship, when they all go so horribly wrong?' Sometimes, when there appears to be no-one to blame for a particular tragedy in our lives, we may even tell ourselves, 'I do not trust God anymore.' Even the very rich and famous still face a lot of disappointments in life. Think of all of those mega-stars whose careers suddenly faded or who went through a series of nasty divorces.

A major disappointment in life can even turn into lasting bitterness or hatred. So many divorced couples end up hating each other, sometimes for decades. We can also end up resenting authority figures because of early disappointments in relation to our own parents. So please explore all your own disappointments in life and do your best to let them go. This will really protect you from falling into a deep depression when your worldly dreams seem to turn to ashes.

Someone who is very depressed has almost no energy whatsoever. If you become depressed, inertia can set in, and you can then shut down on so many levels. You can even opt out of dealing with the basics in life, like paying the bills. Ultimately, an extremely depressed person may entertain suicidal thoughts because they do not even have enough energy to be afraid of dying.

Sometimes, it may even be helpful to push a depressed person to feel anger, because this will raise their vibration a little and give them some energy. Some severely depressed people just cannot motivate themselves to go on living, but angry people can motivate themselves with the energy that anger generates in their system. So occasionally, I will deliberately annoy a very depressed client in order to stimulate more energy in their system.

But I am afraid that if someone has sunk into an extreme depressive state, they may just have to endure being in this hellish state of consciousness for quite some time. Eventually, however, something will naturally shift deep within them, and they will begin to motivate themselves again, like a butterfly finally breaking free from its chrysalis.

Guilt (30)

Guilt is a toxic mix of fear and anger. Whenever we feel guilty, we tend to feel anger towards the person whom we feel guilty about for having treated them badly. We also become afraid that we are going to be punished in some way for our behaviour towards them. Whenever we attack someone, deep down, we will feel guilty, even if we are not consciously aware of this emotion.

Ironically, very fearful, guilt ridden people, who try to cover up their inner pain by attacking others, just end up compounding their guilt. Terrorists are certainly not aware of their deeply subconscious inner guilt. They simply project their guilt outwards and then insist, for example, that Americans are the guilty ones who deserve to be punished or even annihilated. Some terrorists may actually feel a sense of pleasure in torturing and killing others, but underneath this psychopathic veneer, they are in a lot of emotional pain and their violent actions simply compound their hidden guilt.

Guilt is linked to our belief in sin and our perception of a sinful world. Today, we tend to talk about feeling unworthy, rather than being sinful, but this is really just a change of language. Unworthiness may sound like a much softer version of sin, but our belief in our own unworthiness and the concomitant guilt we feel about it, still has extremely negative consequences in our lives.

Guilt is a paralysing type of emotion. Whenever we feel guilty, we tend to want to hide away and not deal with our feelings. Ironically, guilt can often keep us stuck in the same old negative patterns, because our fear and anger are so imprisoning and disabling. So please stop guilt-tripping yourself for any mistakes you may have made in the past. See yourself as having behaved unskilfully, rather than badly, and then simply commit to learning from your mistakes so that you will behave more skilfully in future. If we can rise above our feelings of guilt, and simply see some of our past actions as unskilful rather than bad or wicked, we can move on much more quickly and everyone will benefit.

Shame (20)

Shame is a very deep, dark, life-destroying emotion. When we feel shame, we are buying into the belief that we are innately bad. But when we think this about ourselves, consciously or unconsciously, we can sabotage any chance of finding true love and happiness this lifetime. If we feel ashamed, then deep down we also feel too unworthy to believe that we are loveable.

If you are ready to begin to explore this extremely destructive emotion so that you can lovingly release it, please go into your memories and find a time when you felt ashamed. As you recall that shame, really get in touch with the texture of this particular emotion. Where in your body do you hold shame? When you feel ashamed, what stories are you telling yourself? What thoughts do you believe about yourself when you experience shame? For example, a sexually abused child may grow up believing 'I am dirty,' or 'I am bad'. Deep down, they believe they deserved the terrible things that happened to them. Core beliefs such as these can ruin someone's whole life, unless they are brave enough to correct them with the infinite assistance of a higher, healing power.

But if by any chance you were sexually or physically abused as a child, I strongly recommend you get some expert professional help to process all of your traumatic memories. A higher light can certainly hold you and support you as you work through abuse issues, but the painful memories that may surface can be overwhelming, unless you have a skilled therapist or counsellor to support and guide you through the healing process.

Rising Above Your Negative Emotions

As you advance on your awakening path, one of your key goals should be to sharpen your awareness so that you can observe all of your unexamined assumptions. Once you can observe your personality-self thinking and feeling, without drowning in all its endless dramas, you can create a gap between the core you and your fearful self, and thus start to make some real progress on the path of awakening and healing.

However, we need to be aware that although we may believe that we are spiritually advanced, when we become emotionally disturbed, our energy field will change. It will not matter how well-educated, logical or spiritual we think we are, when jealousy or rage boils up inside of us, we may well throw all our logic and spiritual training out of the window for a while and behave in a very unskilled and hurtful way.

However, the more we raise our consciousness, for example through a regular meditation practice, the more we can utilise all events in our lives, even the most challenging ones, to transcend our stored fear, self-hatred and guilt. Many human beings can become totally trapped in their fearful responses to external events. Their young child dies of cancer, for example, and they are understandably overwhelmed by bitterness and depression for the rest of their life. Some very kind, loving, generous people can sink into an extremely lonely, dark depressed state when terrible things seem to happen to them.

But when we begin to awake, we can rise up above our fearful reactions to the world and then *choose* how we will respond to whatever the world seems to throw at us. We can choose to learn lessons from life, rather than seeing ourselves as life's helpless victims. However, first we have to learn how to rise above our own emotional moodiness.

Most human beings totally identify themselves with their thoughts and feelings. Then they say to themselves, 'Well, this is who I am. This is my life'. But these days, I no longer own all the thoughts and feelings that flow through me. Whenever you say to yourself, 'I am angry,' or 'I am depressed,' you are trapped in a big illusion or bad dream. But as you awake, you will realise that you can always change your mind. You can actually refuse to believe or accept negative thoughts and feelings that inevitably rise up within you from time to time.

Emotions are very obvious. It is not difficult to observe ourselves becoming fearful, sad or angry. But unless we can rise above these emotions, we will still tend to be overwhelmed by them. One very useful trick to assist us to transcend our negative, life-destroying emotions is to use the third person, rather than the first person, as we observe ourselves becoming moody. So, for example, if I observe myself becoming irritated, I now say to myself, 'Jason is getting irritated', or 'Irritation is passing through my system' rather than saying, 'I am really irritated now'.

Of course, when you are talking to someone, it would sound weird to refer to yourself in the third person, but when you are talking to yourself internally, try to develop the habit of avoiding 'I am' when describing your negative thoughts or feelings. For example, you might say something like, 'Oh, Hello anger my old friend, here you are again,' rather than saying to yourself 'I am so angry just now.' Can you see the big difference between these two statements?

You can watch yourself thinking and feeling as though you are watching a third party, and this will immediately put you in the position of being able to distance yourself from life-destroying thoughts and feelings.

If we do not learn to distance ourselves from our moods, we will continue to lash out at others when we are in a rage, and justifiably say, 'I just couldn't help myself'. An extremely angry husband, for example, may even kill his unfaithful wife, and when he then says, 'I just couldn't stop myself. She had to die', he is telling the relative truth. The red mist of his anger and pain completely took him over. He became just like a killing machine that had no control over its lethal actions.

But if you can step back and simply observe your personality-self, you can begin to support yourself and even give yourself helpful advice. Whenever we are stuck in a conflict with someone, we usually feel so fearful and powerless. However, as we start to talk about ourselves in the third person, for example, 'He is really angry today,' or, 'She is very fearful right now,' we can begin to distance ourselves from our feelings. We can thus begin to rise above the belief that we have no choice but to act out our fear or anger by attacking others.

Distancing yourself from your own thoughts and emotions like this will undoubtedly take a lot of the drama out of your life, and even though our dramas tend to be painful, our egos enjoy them. So you have to be very patient with yourself as you learn to live in a far less dramatic, but much more peaceful way. Please do not beat yourself up for still drowning in fear or anger from time to time. Promise to love and support yourself unconditionally, even when you have 'lost it'; just as a loving parent never stops loving their two year old child whilst they are having a terrible tantrum.

Refusing to Play the Role of Innocent Victim

Our personality-selves actually like living our lives as though we were starring in a soap opera full of explosive emotions. We all tend to identify with the hero or heroine figure in the drama that is normal human life. The egoic-self thrives on drama and excitement. It just loves to play the role of self-righteous victim seeking justifiable revenge. But as we advance spiritually, we begin to realise there is something very unnatural about all of this. Then, as we identify more and more strongly with our eternal soul rather than our personality-self, the dramas of this one little lifetime start to seem much less important.

As egos, we love to play the role of helpless, innocent victim persecuted by evil external forces. But in truth, we are never helpless victims of an external world. We are simply trapped by our own fear, guilt and negative beliefs about ourselves and the world. Once we begin to see this, we finally have a real opportunity to let go of and heal all of this incredibly deep and sticky inner pain.

We all have a subconscious mind with deep, negative patterns within it. These negative patterns can then be triggered by external stimuli. For example, your long-standing partner runs off with someone else, and you then feel horrendously jealous because this external event has activated the pre-existing pattern of jealousy deep within your mind. Our subconscious patterns actually determine a great proportion of our reactions to other people and external events in our lives, and we have a *lot* of these patterns deep within our systems.

We usually cannot control our immediate reactions to external events. But we can train ourselves to observe our emotional reactions, rather than allowing them to overwhelm us. Once we learn to do this, we can then explore the programming underneath our habitual reactions to the world around us.

We all now have some negative programming, much of which has been with us since early childhood. Our parents gave us many messages about ourselves as we were growing up – some positive and some negative – and we tended to believe them; what other choice did we have? But believing early negative messages about ourselves can create emotional problems that may last a lifetime. For example, Jane's adoptive mother kept telling her that she was a selfish little girl as she was growing up, and it has taken her over 50 years to begin to shed this quite toxic belief that she acquired about herself.

If you raise your consciousness, and then sit still and observe yourself, you will probably find some similar self-destructive beliefs in your mind, such as, 'I am stupid,' 'I am shy,' or 'I am not worthy of love.' You can also observe that these beliefs not only create fear and confusion in your mind and heart but also influence the way that you experience other people and the world around you.

Bravely Seeing Our Shadow Side

You do have to be strong, courageous and well prepared to see and then release all of your subconscious negative programming that gives rise to negative emotions. Human beings have a very dark side to our psyche, and in extreme circumstances, many of us can act cruelly. For example, in wars, many perfectly ordinary men may rape women from the enemy's side. In civilised societies, we tend to make sure that our shadow-side remains well-hidden, even from our own conscious mind, but as we commit to awakening and self-healing, we have to become conscious of all our inner darkness so we can release it.

Awakening is not all about bathing in love and light. It also involves becoming much more conscious so that you can observe all the dark programming stored in your system. Without looking directly at this programming, we will have no chance of escaping from our past conditioning. When we go to school and listen to our teachers, when we listen to the views of our peers as teenagers and then when we read the papers and watch TV as adults, we are being programmed to become human beings who actually have very little real freedom of thought or action. Most human beings think they have every right to be jealous, angry, or fearful. They do not realise that these negative feelings are slowly destroying them.

As we awake spiritually, we need to keep connecting to an internal observer that can act as a gatekeeper to keep all those life-destroying thoughts and feelings from taking up residence in our minds. As you develop this capacity to calmly observe your own lower mind at work, you will realise you always have a choice. You can always choose letting go, forgiveness, love and compassion instead of guilt, fear, anger, jealousy etc. Most people do not know that they have this choice. They feel jealous, for example, and then they tell themselves an elaborate story to justify their jealousy 100 per cent. They are convinced someone outside of them has caused their jealousy, and unless that person changes their behaviour, they are stuck with their jealousy *ad infinitum*.

But once you are able to watch your lower mind entertaining jealous thoughts and observe your body tensing up with jealousy, you can say to yourself, 'I choose not to entertain these life-destroying thoughts and feelings anymore.'

We all have so much fear and aggressiveness deep within our own minds, and we can only suppress this aggressiveness for so long. This inner aggressiveness is the primary cause of all human conflict, wars, genocide etc. We all like to present ourselves to the world as nice, kind people, but when our pain body is triggered and our aggressiveness is no longer suppressed, we can all behave aggressively.

Rising above a totally self-centred 'me' consciousness and all of our negative egoic emotions is by no means an easy task, but as more and more spiritual pioneers finally achieve it, I am convinced that we will witness a quantum leap forwards for the whole of humankind.

Our Thinking Mind Often Operates Against Us

Our thinking mind is often operating against our highest interests. We want to make more money and then a voice inside our mind says, 'Who are you to be rich and successful?' We long to fall in love and that nasty inner voice says, 'Who on earth would love you?' If you observe your own mind for a while, you will see that part of your own mind is fighting against you. It constantly tells you crazy stories such as, 'Your father/ mother never loved you.'. You suffer so much because you believe these crazy, nasty stories about yourself and others. You are so insecure and unsure of yourself that you even buy loads of expensive things, such as face creams or flash cars, in a vain attempt to boost your low self-esteem.

However, once you simply observe your own thoughts and feelings, and compassionately witness your own suffering, you begin to become less trapped in human fear and darkness. You can, for example, observe what entertaining angry thoughts do to you. You can witness yourself getting angry and then banging a door, breaking a glass, or even attacking another human being.

Please look in the mirror next time you feel really angry and observe its effects on you. Anger weakens your immune system, damages your heart and wrinkles your forehead. Of course your egoic-self gets a big pay-off from being angry, or you would not indulge in it, but there is never a pay-off to anger as far as your true-self is concerned.

The ego always uses anger to try and make someone else feel guilty. An unawakened human being can even convince themselves they hate someone so much that they then plan to kill them. This is so crazy, but your ego really does not want to give up all its paranoid, attacking thoughts and beliefs. So you just have to learn to rise above it into the power of infinite love and light, over and over again, until you are finally free.

The ego thinks anger is powerful. The ego believes that when it gets angry, it can intimidate others and force them to do its bidding or punish them in some way. But in reality, anger has no lasting power. Only love has real lasting power. Unfortunately, in this world we tend to think love is weak and hate is strong, so it may take you several years of spiritual training before you really understand that anger is always a weakness.

Only Love Can Heal Our Toxic Moodiness

Whenever you identify solely with 'me' consciousness, you will inevitably feel fearful. This fear is never logical. It just rises up from deep within you. Your higher mind, on the other hand, dwells constantly in true love and therefore holds no fear whatsoever. This fearless state is our most natural state of being. As you merge your own consciousness with All That Is, everything becomes certain and constant. However, whilst you still have a physical body, you can only reflect this absolute truth, you cannot totally merge with it, because you still need some level of individual consciousness to enable you to continue to function as a physical being in a physical universe.

We cannot suddenly merge our consciousness with All That Is and stay there permanently. We have to move towards this enlightened consciousness step by step. So please start this miraculous process of rising above your negative emotions by vowing to take responsibility for all of your feelings from now on. Don't continue to run away from your negative emotions just because they are painful or uncomfortable. Don't be afraid of your feelings and don't buy into the story you probably tell yourself whenever you are feeling very angry or hurt, that someone has done something to *make* you feel that way.

Please don't 'make the error real'. When you take someone's apparent attack on you personally, you are 'making the error real'. You are buying into the big egoic lie that other people have the power to make you feel a particular way and you are therefore a slave to the vagaries of the world around you.

If someone pushes your buttons, gently move away from that person as soon as you can. You should not do this to avoid your painful feelings, but to give yourself a safe space in which you can calmly observe your feelings, before releasing them into the light.

As soon as you own a feeling that arises in your body and mind, such as jealousy, anger or fear, and say to yourself, '*My* feeling', you are in trouble. So just observe any feeling arising in your system and then calmly sit with it until it subsides. The key to healing all our troublesome feelings is to learn to integrate them, rather than continuing to try to suppress them, or to push them away.

The incredibly good news is that the more we empower ourselves by rising above all of our painful thoughts and feelings, the more we will begin to remove all of our blocks to experiencing the bliss of divine love pouring into every cell of our being. So if you are ever tempted to tell yourself that sitting with your fear or your anger is just too hard to do, please remember that the ultimate goal of this healing practice is for you to become fully aware, at all times, of the infinite love that is your spiritual birthright and your eternal home.

Meditation

All emotions are just energy in motion, and if
I let them flow freely through me, they will do
me no harm.

Sit quietly and feel yourself infinitely supported by a higher light that bathes every cell of your being in bright energy.

Once you feel totally safe and supported by the light, gently bring into your mind a particular fear, past hurt or grievance that you would love to let go of once and for all.

Keep breathing through any discomfort or pain this fear, or fearful memory, triggers within you and ask your intuitive heart, 'Am I now ready to release this emotional pain into the light?'

If the answer is 'Yes', sincerely ask a much higher power to support and guide you miraculously as you go through the rest of this healing meditation.

As you gently open your heart and soften your whole being so that healing energy can flow through you, let your fear or grievance gently drain out of you and down into Mother Earth, or see your painful feelings gently floating upwards and then dissolving into the light.

Feel the peaceful space that arises deep within you, as your stored pain leaves your system.

Now quietly contemplate your future without this self-sabotaging fear and hurt. Sense the freedom, the lightness of being and the innocence that your letting go has created deep within you.

Finally, give thanks for the miraculous healing that you have received through your willingness to face your fear or hurt and then to forgive and let go.

Chapter Four

Higher Levels of Consciousness

Higher Levels of Consciousness

Divinity/Oneness	700 - 1000
Illumination	600 +
Love Energy	540 +
Radiance	500 +
Chi Abundance	400 +
Enthusiasm for Life/Vitality	300 +
Physical Health	200 +

*Created by Jason Chan. Inspired by Dr. David R. Hawkins'
Map of Consciousness*

Empowering Your Personality-Self

Individuals who are currently dedicating their lives to attaining enlightenment are in a very small minority. The vast majority of humanity is just not yet ready to give up its identification with 'me'. Transcending this egoic 'me' self is certainly the most challenging path we can take in this world, but eventually, everyone will see that their egoic-self is dysfunctional – and not even real to boot! However, before you reach this stage of your own awakening and healing journey, I strongly advise you to do your very best to heal and strengthen your personality-self.

Any genuine path to enlightenment is so challenging that first we need to build up our personality-self into an exceptionally strong and fearless character. I always encourage my students to empower themselves and all aspects of their lives before rushing to attain enlightenment. So I strongly recommend that you learn how to be an exceptionally successful and happy 'me' first, before you finally commit to giving up this ultimately illusory identity.

Your 'me' self has been your identity for a very long time, and so you cannot possibly give it up overnight. Time and space are incredibly helpful to those of us who are determined to awake, because they enable us to transcend our egoic-self step by step. Evolution and spiritual transformation need time and space because we cannot clear all the clouds of illusion from our minds in one fell swoop. It would be far too big a shock to our system. We need to raise our consciousness step by step, and the chart at the beginning of this chapter calibrates life-supporting levels of consciousness. I have created it in order to give your left brain something to hang onto, as you begin to explore this transformative process.

Physical Health (200+)

The first level of life-supporting consciousness that we all have to reach is the level related to physical health. Just physical health alone is an incredibly complex subject. The media is now paying a lot of attention to the links between diet and health, but this is only one aspect of an extremely complicated set of issues. Even with an exceptionally healthy diet, someone can still be in a lot of emotional pain and turmoil, and all that emotional and energetic negativity will inevitably damage their long term physical health and well-being.

To cultivate vibrant physical health, younger people should do some regular aerobic exercise, for example jogging or gym workouts, whereas older people are usually better off practising some kind of holistic exercise, such as tai chi, chi kung, or yoga, rather than trying to jog or burning themselves out on tough gym equipment.

If you still want to accomplish something in this world, you will need good physical health and vitality, not just spiritual peace and light! If you just meditate for several hours a day, you can become too detached, or even too spacey, to be of much use in this world. Moreover, if you still need to make a living in this world, or still have worldly dreams to fulfil, you certainly cannot afford to be too chilled out or too weak physically or energetically.

If you are currently in rather frail health or in physical pain, you may have to work hard for quite some time to increase your physical strength and vitality. But please strive for health and vitality out of love for yourself, rather than out of fear of ill-health. Each time you are not sure whether to start exercising, or feel as though you cannot be bothered to cook a healthy meal for yourself, just remind yourself that you are so 'worth it!'

Maintaining good physical health is a very helpful thing to do in our world, whether or not we are consciously following any kind of spiritual path. Whenever you are unwell, you will feel fearful or even depressed and thus become even more self-centred than usual. Just remember how sorry for yourself you felt last time you had a bad cold or the flu!

So striving to be physically healthy and energetically vibrant is not really self-centred. For a start, when you are healthy, your loved ones will not have to worry about you so much. Moreover, if you are inspired to do anything to help this troubled world in any way, you usually need to be in pretty good physical shape to be of any real service to anyone.

Enthusiasm for Life (300+)

The next level of life-supporting consciousness we should all strive to reach is the level at which we start to experience a real enthusiasm for life, linked to an energetic vitality that is an essential aspect of successful living.

Maintaining positive thinking over any length of time requires both physical and energetic vitality. Negative, fearful thinking is almost automatic in the vast majority of human beings, particularly when we are energetically or physically weak. It takes a lot of effort to think positively most of the time. But physical and energetic vitality strongly influence our thinking and mood and can thus give us the feel good factor, regardless of whatever else is happening in our lives.

The mind plays a key role in creating vitality throughout our system. The mind needs to have a spark of life in it in order for us to feel enthusiastic about life. This enthusiasm is fantastic and incredibly good for us. Just think of Anthony Robbins, the American self-help author and motivational speaker. Whenever I listen to one of Anthony Robbins motivational talks, I really believe in myself more. He is truly amazing. His exceptional enthusiasm has inspired millions of individuals to strive for success and to believe that they really can achieve it, whereas so many depressed human beings cannot even motivate their cat.

Of course, in our modern world, there are all sorts of artificial stimulants that can mimic enthusiasm for life. For example, drinking alcohol can give some people a pseudo-enthusiasm for life for a short while, which is why it is so popular. But if you really want to become more passionate about life, raising your energetic vibration, for example through practising Infinite Tai Chi, will give you a natural high that is much safer and longer lasting than an alcohol or drug induced high.

In my twenties and thirties, I was working very hard running my own business, but I noticed that my body was tensing up with all the stress I was feeling. So I took up jogging and ran for over a decade, 4-5 days every week. This really helped me to maintain my vitality for a long time, until I began to age and to lose the spring in my step. Sometimes when I was running, my mind would calm right down, and I would see a light shimmering around trees and other objects. This was a 'Wow!' sensation that only occurred when my energetic vibration was high enough to clear my lower mind so that I could tune into a higher reality.

When I was younger, I noticed that if I did not exercise regularly, I would become more stressed and moody. I also became aware that if my body was tense or weak, it was very hard to think positively. So I now teach the importance of maintaining our physical vitality as long as we possibly can.

Young people have a lot of natural vitality, but they also experience a lot of anxiety and sexual frustration, or too much sexual energy that they then tend to dissipate. Some 25 year olds have already experienced burn out because they have used up too much of their natural 'jing' or vitality. Therefore, even young, vibrant individuals need to learn how to achieve energetic and mental balance and harmony so that they can flow through life, rather than battle their way through it. Older people, on the other hand, need to devote quite a lot of time and effort just to maintain a healthy level of vitality and continued enthusiasm for life.

Chi Abundance (400+)

A sense of aliveness is crucial to our well-being, but sadly most human beings wander around half-dead because they do nothing to top up their energy levels on a regular basis. When your whole being is alive with chi – a life-sustaining force that permeates everything in the entire universe – your physical body will look after itself automatically. When you are full of chi, the seeds of sickness just cannot take root in your mind or body. Moreover, once you are 'chi abundant', your whole life will begin to flow naturally and you will feel connected to the world around you rather than frighteningly separate from it.

So, the first goal that I set for all my students is to reach a state of chi abundance. When we achieve this level of energetic vibration, we become empowered individuals who are more likely to live harmoniously with others. It usually takes my students between 3-4 years of practising Infinite Tai Chi and Infinite Chi Kung to reach this state of chi abundance, but all the time and effort they put in to get there pay massive dividends.

If you are to accomplish anything down here on earth, including spiritual awakening, you will need strong internal energy. Cultivating chi can really begin to raise your consciousness. Ordinary human consciousness, with all its endless fearful thoughts, is far too low for you to make real spiritual progress. You need something strong – like a volcanic blast of energy – to open up your mind and to remove all the heavy clouds in it that obscure the eternal presence of the light.

You also need to cultivate a lot of vibrant internal energy so that you can still your mind and connect to a higher wisdom. Without energy, our mind can become sleepy or it can drift all over the place indulging in pointless fantasies about the future, or useless regrets about the past. But when we have enough internal energy, our consciousness can really expand and then connect to a much higher light that can then pierce through our whole existence to enlighten us on every level.

Whilst you still have any dreams to fulfil in this world, you will need a lot of bright energy, because worldly concerns consume so much of our physical and mental strength. Making money, looking after children, pursuing a career, all these activities can take up a lot of energy, and if we do not take time out to renew ourselves, they can eventually drag us down. So we need to move our bodies mindfully to cultivate chi on a more or less daily basis. Movement gives us life, and without movement, life stagnates.

First, we need to cultivate chi so that we can put our own lives in order. If our own life is a mess, if we are living in poverty or constantly stressed, how on earth can we help our neighbours? If we are exhausted, we cannot even give one other human being a genuine helping hand. We absolutely need strong, harmonious energy to be of any real help in this world.

Then, as we fill ourselves with abundant chi, we become so much more benign and harmonious. We start to be more genuinely co-operative with others, and we begin to rise above all our endless egoic grievances and complaints. I am determined to show as many people as possible how to become chi abundant, so they can become truly alive. I am saddened to walk down the high street and see so many human beings who look as though they are half-dead! If you long for our world to become more peaceful and harmonious, you really do not need to preach peace and harmony to the world, you simply need to go out and teach everyone how to fill themselves up with a very bright, positive energy.

If you are, or long to become, a healer, therapist or mentor of some kind, you definitely need to cultivate real inner strength and exceptionally strong, radiant energy to work effectively and safely with people who are suffering from cancer, a serious addiction of some kind, or a deep depression. Spend some time with a very depressed person, and you will even age more quickly than if you spend your time with someone with a lot of positive energy.

So please be very careful where and with whom you spend most of your time. Irritation with the world, for example, has a strong energy attached to it and so it can be contagious – like flu. If you cannot spend most of your time with high energy practitioners, you can at least raise your own energy and consciousness, particularly through practising holistic forms of exercise, to protect yourself from stress, ageing and other people's negativity.

Ultimately, your inner peace has to become stronger than all the chaos of the world. We live in a world of seemingly endless conflict and confusion. Most people, including possibly some of your own family members and friends, live in a chaotic state of emotional turmoil and angst. You can either sink down to their level and join them in the soap opera they call normal life, or you can commit to practising a serious spiritual art such as meditation, until you become an incredibly strong pillar of light to support others through all the challenges of normal human existence. Eventually, if you want to become truly helpful in this world, your inner peace and sense of well-being has to be stronger than the whole world's collective energy of fear and anger.

Filling our whole being with abundant chi will give us a sense of extreme well-being beyond all positive thinking – which always takes effort. When you are filled with positive chi, you will start to feel naturally fantastic. This is why students on my Infinite Tai Chi courses feel so bright and cheerful after a training weekend. They have not just had a fun time with like-minded friends; they have actually filled up with a life-giving energy that then creates a bubbling internal joy that is so much more effervescent than normal human happiness.

When we have cultivated a lot of chi, being positive is effortless. In fact, it comes as naturally to us as breathing in and breathing out. Moreover, all our endless worries and anxiety disappear for a while, until the chi dissipates once again.

Attaining a state of chi abundance will really assist you tremendously to lead an exceptionally fulfilling, happy life. So please do not settle for anything less. However, it does usually take quite some time and effort to become energetically strong and radiant, because this is a really big leap in human consciousness.

Once you have expanded your energy field and your consciousness, you will find that your point of influence in this world becomes much greater. You will become a truly strong and helpful presence in the world, and everyone who comes into your aura will benefit from your strong, harmonious energy.

However, please note that raising your vibration up to the level of chi abundance only gets you 'half way up the mountain'. You may feel exceptionally healthy and positive at this relatively high level of human consciousness, but you still have a long climb ahead before you will finally transcend all human fear and suffering once and for all.

Cultivating positive energy is a must, but it will not get rid of all of your egoic fear. You can certainly pump yourself up with 'chi power' once you learn how to cultivate chi, and then you may not feel so much fear for a while. However, once you get sick or become frail in old age, all your suppressed fear will simply bubble up into your consciousness once again, unless you have cleared it from the deeper layers of your mind.

So you need to keep raising your consciousness ever higher until you permanently transcend most of the negative side effects of being a human being on planet earth.

Radiance (500+)

Radiance is a state of consciousness between heaven and earth. Once you reach this level of consciousness, your awareness will start to soar up beyond all the heaviness of this world. Radiant consciousness is like bright sunshine. When your mind and body are full of this radiant energy, you can just beam out into the world, like a bright star. When you are radiant, you naturally support life, and everyone around you will be drawn to your exceptionally bright energy. They will then feel much safer and more peaceful in your presence. When you shine out radiantly, you automatically inspire others to raise their own energy and consciousness.

Years ago, I noticed that I was more or less constantly anxious, but when I asked my brain where this underlying anxiety came from, it did not know. Then I became aware that when I meditated, all my personal problems just seemed to disappear for a while, but when I came out of meditation, my problems quickly returned to my awareness. This was very frustrating, until I realised that I also had to train my mind to rise above fearful thinking into radiant thinking.

Radiant thinking, or thinking in the light, is much higher than positive thinking, such as 'Think and Grow Rich'. Radiant thinking has more sunshine energy behind it. Sunshine energy bridges the gap between heaven and earth. Radiance is similar to natural goodness and so when our vibration rises up to this level, we become naturally kind, loving, generous and compassionate, without any effort whatsoever. When we are dwelling in a state of radiance, all our past-programming will start to dissolve. This wonderful state of being also bypasses the lower dualistic mind, with all its egoic notions of good and bad, nice and nasty, virtuous and wicked.

Radiance is potent, pure and exceptionally peaceful. This high vibration corresponds with intuitive knowing and a deep sense of 'All my worldly ambitions are already accomplished'. When you reach this level of consciousness, you will become naturally charismatic, and all your actions will have real power behind them.

However, at this point in human evolution, this fabulous state of being is still rare. In my late 30s, I noticed that I could momentarily achieve a state of radiance, and thus taste the bliss of living miraculously, but at that time, I could not sustain this very high state of consciousness for very long.

After another two decades of diligent practice, I can now attain a state of radiance much more frequently. So now I no longer play small because I know that no-one will benefit, unless I shine my inner light out into the world as powerfully as I can. You too need to shine outwards like a bright star so

71

that people can relate to you as a warm, encouraging, empowering presence in their lives.

Please do not go on playing small, shy, or insignificant. Cultivate exceptional radiance so that you can give others hope and warm support. At the same time, keep filling yourself up with inner peace, compassion and love, until these qualities just ooze out of you and enable you to serve others effortlessly.

If you want to change your life in any way, you have to *be* the change first. You have to become that which you long for. For example, if you still want to attract a loving partner into your life, you probably need to become more loving first or to love yourself more unstintingly.

For quite a long time on your awakening journey, as you try to become more loving or compassionate, you will probably just notice all the negative programming deep in your own mind that is blocking your loving intentions. But once you reach a state of inner radiance, you no longer have to strive to become more loving or compassionate. You will just *be* these beautiful qualities, and then you can simply express this love and compassion in every aspect of your daily life.

Once you reach a very high, radiant state of consciousness, you are so safe! This sense of deep, lasting security will then enable you to become so much more passionate about life. When you are not feeling safe, you simply cannot love life or other human beings, however much you try to do so. You will perceive most human beings as a threat. You will instinctively judge everyone you meet and then justify your negative judgements with your rational thinking. But in a state of radiance, all this fades away and you become naturally non-judgemental and truly compassionate.

In this state, you can accomplish almost anything you put your mind to, as you begin to have a much broader view of life

– as if you were standing on a mountain top and enjoying the panoramic views. From here, you can mould your personality-self so that it will become the perfect tool for your further awakening. You can also effortlessly achieve all kinds of worldly success should you still want it.

I was not born confident and skilled at interacting with other people. But once I raised my consciousness to the level of radiance, I began to mould my personality so that it would serve my soul's purpose this lifetime.

To begin with, as you keep cultivating your connection to love and light, you will just have a glimpse of the state of radiance that can transform your whole being. But if you keep practising Infinite Meditation or a similar kind of energetic/spiritual practice, you will eventually experience incredible internal beauty and brightness that reflect eternity itself.

However, I should emphasise at this point that for some people going up to heaven or experiencing a blissful state of inner peace is really quite easy, whereas staying grounded and secure in this world is very hard work for them. So as our consciousness rises higher and higher, we certainly need to balance raising our awareness with making sure that we are well grounded on Mother Earth. For example, if one of my students starts to feel ungrounded during my courses or retreats, I may advise them to stop meditating for a while and to go for a grounding walk in nature instead. In extreme cases, I may even advise someone that the high energy of our retreats is just not safe for them.

As your calibration keeps rising, you will have more and more opportunities to connect to the light. But please be aware that your consciousness will fluctuate for a very long time. For example, your consciousness may well soar upwards during a spiritual retreat or workshop and then plunge downwards as you go back to your daily life. There is no need to worry about this, just make sure that your overall direction from this day forth is always onwards and upwards.

Once your average calibration rises up to the level of radiance, you will become much more willing to face all of your egoic fear and release it into the light. Your soul will now urge you to explore your inner stored darkness, rather than continuing to hide it under a thin veneer of innocence or niceness. You will also begin to lose your fear of death, and this is quite an accomplishment, because all living beings are instinctively afraid of death, and will usually do everything in their power to protect themselves from facing it.

Eventually, as your consciousness expands further, you will no longer think like the majority of human beings. You will understand how most people operate, but you will no longer agree with them. You will not even agree with them that death is real.

Once you are dwelling in radiant consciousness, your only response to our troubled world will be an impulse to help in any way you can. However, once you reach exceptionally high levels of consciousness in which you are more or less constantly connected to love and light, you no longer have to *try* to help others. Helping others will just arise naturally as you connect to higher guidance and transcendent wisdom.

But to reach this level of spiritual empowerment, you will need to be able to illuminate your whole being in the light, and then to wait – with infinite patience if necessary – until you are inspired by the light to act spontaneously and miraculously.

Love Energy (540+)

Reaching this level of awakening is so important that we are going to devote the whole of the next chapter to it. All you need to know right now is that connecting your individual consciousness to love energy is an incredibly important step on the path to enlightenment. Moreover, connecting to love energy is blissful and can infuse your whole being and your whole life with an out-of-this-world creative power beyond your wildest dreams.

Illumination (600+)

Once your consciousness rises up to the level of illumination, you will naturally bathe your whole being with a higher spiritual light. At this level of spiritual maturity, you will no longer worry so much about any remaining worldly goals you may have. If you just keep pursuing a state of illumination, everything else will be taken care of, because higher consciousness always commands lower levels of consciousness.

Advanced spiritual practitioners can embody a very bright light that corresponds to the celestial realms of existence. But you will need to practise raising your consciousness and energetic vibration very diligently for a very long time before you can gain consistency at this level of illumination. Whenever we engage with the world, we inevitably dim our inner light to some extent, so most genuine spiritual practitioners yo-yo back and forth for a long time, before they are consistently dwelling in a heavenly state of consciousness filled with virtually nothing but light and love.

When your whole being is illuminated, you can ask the light for assistance and then will something to happen for everyone's highest good and it will happen without effort, as long as the right karmic seeds have already been planted.

Even after your consciousness reaches the exceptionally high level of illumination, you may still occasionally experience the frustration of not being able to manifest your soul's highest purpose as quickly as your personality-self might like. Therefore you need to understand, right from the start of your amazing awakening journey, that your timing and divine timing are rarely in synch, and that moreover, your intellectual mind cannot always tell which is which! You may truly believe that you are now totally ready and able to complete your soul's mission this lifetime, but a higher wisdom may know otherwise.

Sometimes, even long-term spiritual practitioners just have to keep cultivating infinite patience and total trust in the process, until all the conditions finally come together for their true purpose in this world to be revealed to them. For example, as Jason Chan (a very temporary personality-self), I still have a somewhat impatient streak. I want to awaken and heal the whole world today! But I now know from many, many years of diligent practice that my timing and divine timing are usually quite different, and so I have learnt to wait patiently for my next soul mission to be revealed to me in God's own perfect time.

When you dwell in the light rather than in egoic darkness, you are so well protected and your mind is so creative, that if you see something wonderful unfolding in your illuminated mind, it's a done deal, however long it may take to manifest in physical reality. When we dwell in an illuminated state of consciousness like this, there is no past or future, only the 'miraculous now.'

If you still want to accomplish great things down here on earth, please do not struggle or stress out. Do not attempt to rely on your own tiny strength to perform miracles. Simply keep raising your individual consciousness to ever higher levels, until you can will something to happen and know, without even a twinge of doubt that it will manifest in this world sooner or later – although not always in the way your lower mind had envisaged.

Once you have raised your consciousness to the level of illumination, you simply need to keep unfolding until you reach the very highest level of consciousness that any human being can attain which we will call 'divinity'.

Divinity/Oneness (700 – 1000)

The source of everything is an indescribable oneness. This oneness is the non-manifest Creator of all things. How much you genuinely aspire to experience this oneness will determine whether or not you finally attain this exceptionally high level of being that lies beyond all duality and all illusions. But please know that once you attain this ultimate level of human consciousness, everything you do will be imbued with God's Presence.

God never hides from any of His children. Of course, God is not a specific being, but the indescribable Source of all that is, but because our human minds cannot comprehend this, we still have to talk about God in human terms. As a child of God you already know Him so well, but in this world, you have to really calm your mind, open your heart and raise your vibration to a very high level, before you can dwell in His divine oneness.

Ultimately, you will only move your mind out of this oneness in order to selflessly serve your brothers and sisters who are still dwelling in painful duality. But even as you do this, you will know that nothing else really exists except this absolute truth, and so now you will not mind if your personality-self dies away, because you will identify with your true-self, rather than your personality and physical body. You will no longer fear physical death because you will know without a shadow of a doubt that you are not a physical being.

Your true-self is all powerful, whereas your personality-self, until you awake, is a helpless slave to the dream world it inhabits. But please understand that as long as you still have a physical body, you cannot hold an awareness of total oneness for too long. Divine oneness expands into infinity and vibrates at such a high level that it is impossible for any physical being to embody it for more than relatively short periods of time. The very highest level of vibration that a human being can sustain whilst remaining on this planet calibrates at 1000. However, once an extremely advanced spiritual practitioner has left their physical body, they can expand much further than this in higher realms of existence.

Please understand that there are different degrees of enlightenment and that experiencing a moment or two of divinity or oneness during a deep meditation does not mean that you are now totally enlightened. But when you merge your consciousness into oneness, even just for a moment or two, you will be very aware of God's Presence. Your lower mind will still have no idea about the true nature of God and reality, but your intuitive open heart will know God intimately. In this state of enlightened grace, your lower mind does not move, and so you can dwell for a while in 'All That Is' and simply connect to God's Infinite Grace.

Ultimately, we can transmute all physical matter into spiritual matter so that we no longer feel trapped in a relatively gross, dark physical world. As you keep connecting to the light, your internal 'light bridge' will become stronger and stronger, until you can much more easily live your life in divine grace, rather than struggling endlessly through life like Sisyphus.

Throughout the ages, from day one, human beings have found life on earth a terrible struggle. Even today, when so many of us have running hot water, plenty of food and excessive amounts of clothing, we all struggle so much! Please do not go on living like this. Vow to become a pioneer of radiant living and thus pave the way for others to find true inner peace and freedom.

The vast majority of human beings simply cannot tune into divinity. You need exceptional dedication to your chosen spiritual path before you can reach this incredibly high level of consciousness. But when you finally totally surrender your little personality-self and temporary physical existence into divine power, you are almost home.

Surrendering to the divine is never passive. It takes both a truly devotional heart and a very strong spiritual will, but there is also spiritual grace in this active, dynamic form of surrender. Once you can surrender completely into the divine, you will gain true life and this life is eternal and invincible.

At this miraculously high level of consciousness, you will become more and more aware of God's will or Divine will, and your egoic-self will become less and less significant to you. But even very advanced spiritual practitioners notice egoic self-centred thoughts are still there from time to time, trying to stop them attaining absolute enlightenment.

The ego will inevitably keep trying to capture all of your spiritual experiences so that it can use them to aggrandise itself. As your consciousness rises up to an exceptionally high level, the egoic voice in your head will whisper 'You are *so* spiritual!' This is a big temptation, or trap, advanced practitioners need to avoid, if they are not to sabotage their further spiritual growth.

Even at the highest levels of spiritual practice, your further awakening or enlightenment is a big threat to your egoic-self, and so at virtually every level on the awakening path, you will experience resistance to further healing and awakening. Moreover at first, as you rise upwards and connect to the light, this light will illuminate previously hidden layers of fear and darkness in your mind and so even advanced spiritual practitioners can go through periods of time during which they experience a load of fear.

Your core aim at this very high level of spiritual practice however is to think, feel, love and shine outwards like a saint or bodhisattva. Great saints in this world have a brilliant presence emanating from their soul. Their divine presence can even continue to uplift humanity long after their physical presence has gone. All saints emanate the very high vibration of divinity, but in their own unique way. Their divine presence miraculously inspires all awakening souls, and in particular, those disciples or followers who can directly tune into their exceptionally high, divine energy field.

Saints do not have to *do* anything in this world. Their miraculously high consciousness and energy will do everything through them. Mother Meera (whose followers believe her to be an embodiment of the Divine Mother), does not need to speak to anyone to communicate with them. She simply holds divinity in her aura at all times and then silently blesses all who attend Darshan with her. We are so blessed to have one or two great beings like this down on earth with us. They are like extremely bright stars in a very dark sky, lighting our way home to the ultimate truth.

However, I must emphasise that if a few exceptionally dedicated spiritual practitioners can shine like guiding stars in our troubled world, so can we. We just need to have complete trust in our chosen spiritual practices and complete dedication to our own awakening and healing path. We need to vow that, as God is our witness, we *will* climb to the very top of the path 'up the mountain' and beyond, step by step by step, until we too are a miraculous, illuminating, healing presence in the midst of so much worldly darkness.

Meditation

Divine light fill me
Divine light guide me
Divine light transform all my
weaknesses into strengths

Sit quietly and consciously take a few deep, calming breaths.

Place your right palm over your left palm facing your dantien (2 fingers down from your naval). Imagine a very bright golden flame at your dantien and breathe in and out about nine times with your focus on the flame at the dantien. See, feel or imagine this flame growing brighter and stronger with each breath that you take.

Bring your palms up to hold a 'golden sun' in front of your solar plexus. Focus your mind and your breath on your solar plexus for about nine breaths and see, feel or imagine the golden sun growing bigger and brighter with every breath that you take until your whole solar plexus is filled with golden sun energy.

Bring your palms up at the side of your chest facing upwards. Focus gently on your heart centre and imagine it opening up like a beautiful flower as you breathe a very bright light from all directions into it for around nine breaths.

Spend the rest of this 15-20 minute meditation gently focussing on your open, illuminated heart.

Chapter 5
The Power of Love

The Transformative Power of Love

Do you have any idea of the power of love? You may think the saying 'love can move mountains' is just hyperbole, but I have to tell you that it is the ultimate truth.

Unfortunately, in the valley of normal human consciousness, love is often seen as a weakness rather than a strength because most human beings just do not understand true love, and so we very often confuse love with neediness or desire. Normally, when we say we are in love, what we really mean is that we desperately want someone. But love energy or love consciousness, (calibrating at 540+) is about *being* not wanting.

The more you dwell in love energy the more your whole personality-self will be transformed. You will become wiser and gentler, and you will have far less need to go out into the world to seek for satisfaction. You will feel so safe that you will automatically become much more benign. You will naturally be warm and friendly towards everyone and others will instinctively feel that they can trust you.

However, we have to feel exceptionally safe to love truly. Love is in the air, but if your consciousness is not high enough, you won't experience this universal love. If you are just a little anxious, you cannot dwell in love because love and fear simply cannot co-exist. Without dwelling in true love, you can only cope, in the best way that you know how, with living in fear.

In this physical universe, we are all loveless because physical matter is not made of love. Our universe is amazing. Just gaze at the stars for a while – Wow! But it is still lacking in love. Another big problem with our universe is that nothing we perceive with our five physical senses will last. The temporary nature of all physical life is a big, fearful puzzle for us.

When you realise, for example, that you love your children so much, and yet you can do nothing to prevent them suffering, you will probably panic. You will also panic whenever your body gets sick and reminds you of its total vulnerability and impermanence.

In fact, whenever you are concerned about any aspect of your body, you are reinforcing the belief 'I am a body', and this belief inevitably makes you anxious. If you keep focussing your attention on your toes for example, you will be incredibly upset if your toes are cold or if you notice a fungal infection in your toenail.

Before your awakening, not only do you totally identify yourself as a physical body, you also really believe, whether consciously or subconsciously, that you can be abused, abandoned and betrayed. Unfortunately, when you hold beliefs like these in your mind, this is what you will eventually experience in your life. Then you will say, 'Oh God, why me?' 'Life is so unfair. Every time I love someone I get so hurt!' But it is your own beliefs that are causing you to suffer, not God. For example, if you believe that someone you love so much can abandon you, you are secretly asking to be abandoned. You might as well put a sticker on your forehead with 'Abandon me!' emblazoned on it. But I advise you not to tell others this truth about life or they will probably hate you for it.

However, when you learn to raise your consciousness high enough to dwell in true love, you will naturally extend love out into the world around you, and then you will know without a doubt that your true-self can never be abandoned or betrayed. When you dwell in love energy, you will feel so safe. You will also create an exceptionally bright energy field around you that will attract very positive events and people into your life.

But in order to utilise the awesome power of true love, we first need to get in touch with the high energy of love's essence and then become familiar with it. I cannot really describe or define this love for you, but when you connect to it, for example in a deep meditation, you will just know it. Then you will also know the difference between everlasting love and temporary, human love that always comes and goes.

Occasionally, unawakened human beings do experience unconditional love for a parent, partner, child or very close friend – at least for a short while – and this love is exactly the same love that a saint or bodhisattva extends to everyone. The big difference is that the saint's love is unchanging, whereas normal human love can so quickly turn to anger or even hate.

Whenever we love someone unconditionally, we will support them with everything we have. This unconditional commitment in turn creates real power, and we can use the power of this selfless love to support every aspect of our own lives and the lives of others.

Unconditional love can uplift, motivate and even heal the sick, because it is a selfless state of consciousness. Tuning into unconditional love always makes us bigger and brighter. In this love, we can transcend all our self-centred egoic desires, without feeling as though we are sacrificing anything of any real value. When you know the bliss of dwelling in unconditional love, you will no longer need to cling to another body or personality because you 'love' them, and so dwelling in true love will bring you great freedom and peace of mind.

Please commit to connecting to the power of love to make all your dreams come true this lifetime. Extend love into any aspect of your life and watch it transform as if by magic! If we do everything with love and nothing but love in our hearts and minds, we cannot fail.

Unfortunately, I know that however much you long to do so, you probably cannot love the whole wide world unconditionally yet, because you do not yet completely and unreservedly love and accept yourself. So, one of your core tasks, as you awake, is to begin to heal your deep sense of unworthiness so that you can know just how loveable you truly are. As you do this, your whole life will be transformed and problems that previously seemed insurmountable will simply melt away, without any conscious effort to solve them on your part. I guarantee it.

Lack of Love is a Killer

The Western world's number one killer is heart disease, not cancer. From a spiritual perspective, heart disease is actually linked to our deep down belief in our lack of love. We all feel, consciously or subconsciously, as though we lack love and most of us have closed our hearts up against the pain of falling in and out of love, or the agony of unrequited love, and so we all suffer.

We all grow up deprived of unconditional love and then we tell people, 'I'm OK'. But I have to tell you that you are not OK! You are just coping with all of your accumulated emotional pain and you probably have some kind of chip on your shoulder. Most people are so full of emotional pain, whether they consciously realise it or not, that they just have to project their pain outwards and get angry with the world. Alternatively, they may try to suppress their emotional pain by stuffing it down into their physical body, and then they may well become physically sick for no obvious reason.

Many people even die because they are love-deficient. Butter is not really a killer. In the American TV series CSI, they do not arrest butter week after week for the mass murder of middle-aged Americans. When someone dies of heart disease, from a deep, spiritual perspective, we can say that they are dying from a lack of love.

When we tense ourselves up in fear, the muscles around our heart become tight and then they can become weak, and so our hearts will become tired, particularly as we grow older. So, we urgently need to learn how to open our hearts and connect to true love, in order to restore our natural inner strength and harmony and to prolong our precious physical existence.

When you tense up against life and your heart beats too fast, you may well shorten your lifespan. But if you slow down and allow your heart to beat more slowly, you will probably live longer. Long-term meditators have a slow heartbeat and so they tend to live longer than non-meditators. They do not race around frantically. They learn to slow down and 'smell the roses'. They also practise filling their hearts and minds with love and gratitude on a daily basis.

Sometimes, when I am doing a Ling Chi healing on a client, I remove heavy particles of energy from around their heart. I become an energetic heart surgeon, removing energetic blockages around someone's heart. I then channel love and light into my client's heart to strengthen and protect it. As an experienced energy and spiritual healer, I am very aware of how closed and wounded most people's hearts are and how urgently they need to open and heal them.

Opening Your Heart to Love

If you keep raising your vibration until you reach the level of unconditional love, I promise you your body will no longer age so quickly and you should suffer a lot less ill health. Vibrant good health is actually a wonderful side effect of living our whole lives in love. But the emotional benefits of connecting to love energy are even more spectacular, as we experience the indescribable joy of true love deep within our heart and mind.

Unfortunately, not many human beings yet live their lives from their open heart centres. Their energy still tends to be stuck in their three lower centres. However, as more and more individuals discover the energetic and spiritual tools that will open their hearts to true love, we will eventually find ourselves living in a much more peaceful and kind world. But first, we all have to learn how to connect to the love that already lies deep within us, rather than hopelessly searching for it in the external world. We also have to acclimatise ourselves to the power of love!

We all long for love, but we have become so used to living in a loveless state that we can now only take so much love at any one time. Until you get used to dwelling in love, you will probably just have a glimpse of it and then find some reason to stress yourself out once again, so that you can go back to a much more familiar – but pretty loveless – state of being.

You are like someone who has dwelt for decades in a very gloomy cave who is suddenly exposed to bright sunlight. At first, you can only stay in the light for a very short time before retreating back into the gloom. Initially, opening our hearts to love tends to make us feel so vulnerable that we instinctively close them up again quite quickly. We are all living in a relatively loveless world. We learn to cope, in fact we become coping geniuses, but this is a human tragedy, because no one can truly thrive in a world lacking in love.

Sometimes, as our heart centre begins to open, it is such a shock to our system that we may even experience a severe heartache.

So please don't panic if you experience an aching in your heart after some kind of major spiritual opening. This heartache reflects the releasing of deep inner loneliness based on our belief that we are living in a loveless world. But once you connect to the high vibration of true love, you will be able to feel love flowing through your whole being, and your heart will naturally open up in this blissful energy field.

Once we connect to true love, our whole life can become a true joy. When we devote ourselves to connecting to this love day in and day out, all our worldly affairs will be completely taken care of by its miraculous energy. You can devote everything that you do to 'Love' – which is actually another name for God. For example, you can do the dishes and devote this humdrum activity to 'Love'. Don't listen to your endless thoughts so much. Don't try so hard to be clever or sophisticated. Just dwell in love energy throughout your days and watch miracles unfolding in front of your very eyes.

Divine Love is Infinitely Powerful

Please understand that divine love is infinitely powerful! Becoming devoted to this love will automatically start to heal and empower all aspects of your life.

If you combine love with sunshine energy, the world is your oyster. Just begin each day by stilling your mind, connecting to love and light, and then extending this love and light out into the day ahead. At first, you may have to utilise your imagination to do this, but if you keep practising diligently, you will eventually be able to extend real love and light out into your world without even having to think about it.

Once you can embody love energy and then extend it out into the world around you, you can bless all of your nearest and dearest with unconditional love, and they will begin to feel more secure in the world. Extending unconditional love to your children, for example, is a wonderful way to protect them. But please understand that your children have to learn their own life lessons, and once they are adults, you just have to set them free to make their own mistakes so that they can mature and evolve.

Remember that love and fear cannot co-exist, and so whenever you are worrying about your family members or friends, you are bathing them in the life-destroying energy of fear, rather than the life-supporting energy of love. I know that it is virtually impossible for a mother or father to stop worrying about their children, even when their children are in their forties, but if you have children, each time you notice yourself worrying about them, please smile gently to yourself and then do your very best to release all your anxiety into the light.

Extending unconditional love to all of your friends and relatives is a beautiful practice. But to do this effectively, you will first have to master the art of spiritual forgiveness. For example, you will need to release all of your grievances against your parents from your mind and heart, before you can remember just how much you have always loved them. Our stored grievances block our awareness of the unconditional, deep love we always have for one another. Moreover, all our stored grievances are like accumulated silt that blocks the flow of life-giving water through a pipe, and so unless we clear all of these grievances from our system, we will not be a completely clear channel for love to flow through us and then out into the world around us.

Make Love the Motivation for Everything that You Do

We all need to find a deep and lasting positive purpose to our lives, or we will lose vitality and age prematurely. Eventually, we may even sink into apathy or depression. You should always be eager to jump out of bed in the morning. Your life should have a real purpose that fills you with enthusiasm, as though you were getting up each morning to meet your lover.

The highest and most inspiring motivation for achieving anything in this life, including spiritual enlightenment, is always love. When you really love someone, you will devote so much time and energy to them. You will cross the widest ocean to spend just one night with the one you love so much.

So please be good to yourself and train your mind to love life in all its wondrous manifestations. Find someone or something to love every day, and make love the core motivation for everything that you do. Then, spend as much of your time as you possibly can doing what you really love; activities that make your heart sing.

If you go to work primarily to earn money, you will be lukewarm about your job, even if you are earning £100,000 plus a year. Making money is really not a good motivation for doing anything. My advice is always 'Love the work you do, love your colleagues, and love your clients or customers'. Loving your work, and those whom you serve through your work, will give you so much more vitality, focus and passion, than working primarily for your own financial security. If you do a job you really love, it will even keep you young and radiant year after year.

If you are going to spend a lot of time with someone, again make sure you love them. This does not mean that you have to like everyone whom you spend time with, but it does mean you should try and avoid spending a lot of time with someone solely out of guilt or loneliness. Insist on spending most of your time with those with whom you can exchange loving energy and true kindness.

You do not need to be in romantic love with someone to exchange love energy. In fact, it is often easier to exchange true love with really good friends than with a sexual partner, because sexual intimacy tends to bring up all sorts of unhealed issues for most of us. But once you can connect to the high vibration of true love, you should always try to spend as much time as possible with others who are dwelling in the same universal love, because these exceptional individuals will naturally support your further personal and spiritual evolution.

Fall in Love on a Daily Basis

I dearly hope that you have experienced the bliss of falling in love at least once in your life. Falling in love is one of the best parts of the package of being human. When Jane fell in love for the first time in her 20s, she noticed that the grass was much greener and the sky much bluer than before!

When we are in love, we can focus exclusively on our loved one with great intensity. When we momentarily join with our beloved, we feel truly alive. The whole troublesome world seems to disappear whenever we gaze into the eyes of the one we love. If you are not convinced, just go to a busy airport and watch two lovers saying goodbye or hello to one another, totally oblivious to the tension and chaos all around them.

You certainly do not have to wait until you meet the man or woman of your dreams to fall in love. If you train your mind to focus intensely on any object, you can then feel as though you are joining with it, and so you can fall in love with it. You can fall in love with a tree in this way, or a flower, or a piece of music. You simply have to open your heart and focus one-pointedly on something until you merge with it, because true joining and true love are basically the same. Of course, this does take some mind-training to achieve, but every effort you make to increase your ability to focus lovingly on something until you fall 'in love' with it is definitely worth it.

Love touches our hearts and stimulates them to open up like beautiful flowers in bright sunlight. So please do not wait for your soul mate to come along to fall in love. Fall in love every day of your life. Love is everywhere. Love is in the air we breathe. You just have to learn how to tune into its blissful high energy. When you really know love is absolutely everywhere just waiting for welcome, you will no longer need to grab hold of someone and keep their body close to yours to try to assuage your loneliness.

However, in order to experience this infinite and eternal love, we have to meet certain conditions. Our egoic-self cannot really love. It can only strongly desire someone and then believe that this is love. So, if we truly long to tune into the energy of love on a daily basis, we need to learn how to rise above our egoic self-centredness into a much higher level of consciousness.

Your Soul Longs Only for True Love

Your personality-self has a hundred and one desires, but your soul only wants to dwell in love, because then, and only then, it is totally free. However, you will not be able to open your heart fully to love, until you strengthen your lower energy centres, particularly your base centre. If this centre is weak, tense or blocked, you will inevitably feel insecure and fearful because the base centre is linked to survival and security issues. Then, if you feel at all anxious or fearful, you cannot experience true love, because love and fear can never co-exist in our consciousness.

Once you strengthen your three lower centres – for example through practising one of my Infinite Chi Kung sequences such as *Standing like a Tree* – you will find it much easier to open your heart to love. Opening up to love will enable your whole being to flourish. So please make a real commitment to live your life in love from this day forth. Only you can determine that from now on, you are going to do everything in your power to live your life in love. Can your mother do this for you? Of course she can't! No one else can lead your life for you and so finding true love is 100 per cent your responsibility.

Will you be able to live your whole life in love just by making a commitment to do so? No! We are so used to living in fear that it will usually take us a lot of time and effort before we completely change our minds and fully open our hearts to dwell in love all of the time. But please never give up your quest for true love. It is the only worthwhile quest in the whole wide world!

When you are dwelling in love energy, the whole world becomes a happier place, thanks to you. If on the other hand, you are determined to remain fearful and miserable for the rest of your life, everyone around you will suffer, including your cat or your dog. So please never assume pursuing love and happiness is a selfish goal. Truly happy individuals, who simply refuse to let any external circumstances disturb their connection to love energy, are a miraculous blessing to the whole world.

Needy Attachment is Not True Love

No other human being can love you unconditionally 24 hours a day. We long for others to love us and most of us are desperate to find a special 'someone to love', but as soon as a loved one annoys us, our love for them tends to fly out of the window and vice-versa. It is quite irrational, and even insane, to keep looking for true love in all of the places where it can never be found. Loving a cat or a dog is usually much easier for us than trying to love another human being, and yet most people, especially young people, still believe that the perfect human love partner is out there somewhere.

You need to cultivate tremendous self-discipline and tolerance to live closely with another human being for any length of time. To be able to live harmoniously with even one other person, first and foremost you need to have an exceptionally good loving relationship with yourself. If you cannot love yourself 24/7, what on earth makes you think someone else can provide the love you are withholding from yourself?

Most human beings, rather than learning to love themselves unconditionally in order to fill up their inner sense of lack, still fearfully attach themselves to another human being and then 'love' them in a dangerously possessive way. If their partner flirts with someone else at a party for example, they inevitably feel horribly jealous. If their partner of twenty or thirty years ups and leaves them, they will be devastated. Some people even become attached to their most prized possessions such as their Rolex watch. They say to themselves 'This is *my* beautiful watch. I just love it,' and then they are distraught if somebody steals it.

If you need to possess another human being, or a lot of expensive things, in order to feel loved or secure, you are in big trouble, because nothing in this world lasts. In fact, you do not even possess your own body, let alone someone else's body. You just lease your physical body from Mother Earth for a while. You should certainly do your best to look after your physical body whilst you have one, but if you become too attached to it or 'love' the way it looks, you will suffer sooner or later, when your body weakens and then dies.

Dying is so stressful for most human beings because they know that they cannot take their loved ones, or any of their precious possessions, with them. But if you long for lasting freedom and happiness, you need to understand that needy attachments are the opposite of true love and so they can never bring us the lasting satisfaction that we seek.

Dwelling in Love Energy

Love is everywhere. But you have to learn to open your mind and heart to enable this out of this world energy to illuminate you, so that you can feel much more genuinely alive and truly empowered.

Many people in our stressful modern world try to feel more alive by getting an instant boost from something like alcohol or drugs. Following an awakening path back home to love will probably take us a lot longer before we experience that totally alive feeling, but it is so worth it! Whenever you are dwelling in love energy, you automatically feel so alive. Being in love always feels so good, so why not insist that you will do everything in your power to discover how to dwell in love all of the time?

Every soul in this world is longing to connect to unconditional, all embracing love, but most human beings simply do not know what it is. They believe love is just an emotional feeling, but real love is actually a very high energy that extends infinitely and indiscriminately to support all of life in its trillion different disguises.

When you dwell in love, every cell in your body is fully alive, your mind is clear and quiet and you simply know. Know what? You know the miraculous truth about life. But this statement really will not make much sense to you until you experience the miraculous truth directly. When you connect to this truth, you really do not want to think, because whenever you think, you will pull your vibration down from the level of pure love and light.

When you are bathed in love energy, your whole body may well buzz with joy and you may even feel goose bumps tingling up your spine. This is just one indication that love energy is pouring through you.

I do hope that you experience love energy pouring through you at least once in your life. My prayer for you is that you will soon experience this incredible love every day of your life. Love energy is so awesome that once you experience it, even for a moment or two, you will just long for more and more of it. I am totally addicted to love energy. It is one of the very best sensations this life has to offer us, and we do not even need a partner to experience it. In fact, unless your partner has an exceptionally high vibration or consciousness, they will probably not be capable of sharing true love energy with you.

How to Connect to Love Energy

To experience love energy, we have to raise our vibration way above the average level of human consciousness. Given that, according to Dr David R. Hawkins, the majority of human beings' calibration is still less than 200, you can see that raising our average vibration up to 540+, the level I have assigned to love energy in my chart of higher human consciousness, is quite a challenge, but one that a number of my long-term students have now achieved.

You will certainly need to take up some kind of regular spiritual practice to raise your vibration above the level of intellectual thinking and into the realm of genuine spiritual experiences, including the experience of being bathed in divine love. Even the most brilliant intellect cannot know the energy of divine love because the vibration of normal human thinking is just too low to experience its high vibration.

Professor Stephen Hawking for example, has a truly brilliant mind, but he is a scientist, not a spiritual practitioner, and so he is convinced God does not exist, because science cannot find any proof of God's existence. We actually need to have a subjective experience of God's love to know God exists. I do not believe in God. I *know* God because I have gone beyond my thinking mind to experience His infinite love directly with my whole being.

Sadly, most people in our world are living relatively loveless lives, and to date, only a very small minority of individuals have connected to love energy for any significant length of time. Most human beings are still imploding with fear and anger because of their low level of consciousness. Tensing up fearfully against the world is very normal, but when we tense up like this, we inevitably close our hearts, and then we experience living in fear, rather than love. The majority of human beings live all their lives in fear and lack rather than true love, and so we have far more thieves and con artists in our world than saints. Saints love all living creatures unconditionally. But this approach to life is definitely still 'the road far less travelled'.

Whilst you are dwelling in the energy of love, for example during a very deep meditation, you will know that everything is possible. But when you come back into thinking mode, you will start to judge and evaluate everything and everyone once more, and then all that beautiful love energy will dissipate, as your vibration falls back down to the level of normal, fearful human consciousness.

It takes a lot of disciplined practice to open our hearts and minds fully to love energy, and then to be mindful enough to stop our habitual, fearful egoic programming from pulling us back down to fear once again. But eventually, if we keep practising opening our hearts to love, we can dwell in love energy virtually all of the time.

Flowing Harmoniously in Love

If you long to live your whole life in love, please practise flowing harmoniously with life, instead of tensing up against it. Do some kind of holistic exercise every day or go for a mindful walk in nature to tune into the beautiful flow of life. Then, just keep raising your consciousness up to ever-higher levels, until you really love all of life, and can live your whole life in love, rather than succumbing to the much lower energies of chronic anxiety and stress.

This is not yet a peaceful planet. It is still full of hatred, conflict and confusion. But when you learn to flow through life with love in your heart, life can be so beautiful! When you finally flow like this, you will feel so well-protected, even in the midst of chaos. When you are dwelling in love, your energy will be radiant and then everything you do in life will become a joy. Cleaning your house, driving your car, taking the dog for a walk, will all become blissful activities, as you flow harmoniously, breathe consciously, move mindfully, and truly love each and every moment of your life.

Please do not dampen down your natural aliveness. Do not turn your back on the love that is the very essence of your true-self. Those who mainly seek for comfort or physical pleasure in life, for example by drinking loads of alcohol or stuffing themselves with chocolate or pizza, are not truly alive. If you just go for comfort or physical pleasure for the rest of your life, you will look back over your life when you are dying and you will be sorely disappointed. But when you are totally centred in divine, everlasting love, you can even witness your own physical body dying and know you are perfectly safe.

Everything in this world that is truly alive flows. Think of the difference between a flowing river and a stagnant pond. When you flow in a never-ending stream of love, you can master the art of living radiantly through all the ups and downs of daily life. You can create a graceful, powerful flow of radiant, loving energy wherever you go in life, and then you will naturally create true beauty around you for others to admire and enjoy.

When my most advanced students perform Infinite Tai Chi, they are actually 'love in movement' for a while, because as they move, they still their thinking mind, connect their consciousness to love energy, and flow naturally with true grace and strength. When one of my advanced students performs Infinite Tai Chi with supreme focus, observers can be moved to tears.

My Infinite Tai Chi Form is not a martial art, nor is it just slow, gentle movement. It is a spiritual art. It is 'Movement in the Light' or 'Movement in Love Energy'. Practising a holistic art such as Infinite Tai Chi, even at the foundational level, can really assist you to become radiant, and once you reach this level of consciousness, it is so much easier to then raise your consciousness to the level of love energy so that you can dwell in love throughout your day.

When our mind, body and emotions flow together in perfect harmony, we will get in touch with a universal life force that can assist us to feel truly alive and in love in each and every moment. Then, once we are flowing harmoniously with life, we will inevitably attract more love into our lives. But this love is not at all the same thing as sexual chemistry or physical desire that comes and goes. True love has a permanent, unchanging aspect to it. This true love never comes or goes. It is only our awareness of it that changes.

Meditating in Love Energy

Some types of meditation are really just an effective form of relaxation. This type of meditation is still very good for you and may even help you to reverse the ageing process. But relaxation and stress relief are not the main aims of my Infinite Meditation. In Infinite Meditation, we still our bodies and calm our minds, but we also raise our energetic vibration so that we can experience dwelling in true love for a while.

Stilling your mind and opening your heart so that you can connect to the very high energy of true love will give you a supreme sense of well-being. Connecting to love in one of our group meditations certainly seems to bliss out many of my students. However, our ultimate goal is not simply to feel blissful for a while. We are aiming to return home to love and to stay there permanently.

If you are now ready to take the universal journey back home to love, you do need to be aware that your egoic-self does not want you to take this journey. The egoic thought system is primarily an unconscious thought system, but it nevertheless traps most of us in a loveless state of mind.

The egoic thought system, that has invaded your mind like a corrupting virus, does not want you to rise above it so that you can observe it and see just how nasty and destructive it really is. It sees your determination to awake as a real threat to its continuing existence. So it will insist that you cannot meditate, or sit still in love for 30 minutes twice a day. No! If you cannot sit to meditate, this means that you do not yet *want* to do it, rather than you can't.

The good news is you can train your personality-self to rise above its resistance to meditating. You can programme yourself to sit still for a while each day, whether your personality-self wants to or not, until it eventually becomes an automatic habit – like brushing your teeth.

If you are going to be addicted to anything in life, please become addicted to meditating in love. Become addicted to the bliss of meditating in an infinite, unconditional love that is eternally waiting for you to connect to it. When your consciousness rises up to the level of unconditional love, miracles will happen quite naturally, and all your normal personal problems and frustrations will disappear; at least for a while.

Unfortunately, when you are not used to receiving a lot of love, connecting to the intense energy of true love can feel quite uncomfortable after a while. If you experience God's love as some kind of threat – consciously or more likely subconsciously – you will inevitably do something to lower your consciousness down to a loveless level once again, soon after having tasted the bliss of bathing your whole being in love's essence.

So at first, as you learn to meditate, you need to focus on strengthening your three lower energy centres, so that you can feel really safe, strong and balanced. Then, and only then, you can begin to open your heart centre to experience love energy pouring into and through your whole being.

Extending Love to the Whole World

Once you have attained and maintained the very high level of consciousness you will need to dwell in love energy, you will eventually be able to do everything in your life with loving kindness and compassion.

You can commit to extending loving kindness and compassion out into the world at all times, without necessarily *doing* anything at all. Lots of very intelligent and well-meaning individuals work tirelessly trying to make our world a better place and I salute them! However, if we sit quietly and raise our consciousness to the level of love energy, we can bless the world without rushing around like headless chickens trying to fix all of the world's endless problems.

When we can connect our individual consciousness to love energy, we will become genuinely compassionate. Cultivating true compassion in turn helps us to transcend all our egoic beliefs about good and bad, and even enables us to forgive the perpetrators of terrible atrocities, as we say to ourselves, 'They do not know what they do,' or, 'They must be in so much emotional pain and turmoil to do such terrible things'.

Saints and bodhisattvas do not just have compassion for all of the world's victims, they also extend love and compassion to all of the perpetrators of violence in the world, because they fully understand that these 'aggressors' simply cannot help behaving violently. Their level of consciousness is just too low for them to exercise any real choice over their 'evil' behaviour.

In any case, saints and bodhisattvas always see the bigger picture. They know worldly power never lasts, and that even the most powerful, vicious dictators and genocidal maniacs lose all of their dark, egoic power, sooner or later. They also understand that even the most vicious of violent perpetrators is simply a child of God seeking for love in the most unskilled ways imaginable.

Please do your very best not to condemn as evil those who do terrible things out of a lack of love. For example, do your best not to hate any terrorists who may be plotting to bomb your city or your country. When we are lacking in love, we can all act in horribly unskilled ways, but this does not make us evil. It simply means that we are temporarily insane.

When we finally rise above our own egoic insanity and re-discover the love that is the essence of our core being, our only response should be a hymn of gratitude and a determination to assist our fearful brothers and sisters to connect to the miraculous love that is awaiting them too.

As you awake and spend more and more of your time dwelling in love, you will notice that you no longer have such a strong urge to go out into the world to find love or to satisfy your personality-self's endless desires. You will also notice that your automatic response to those who perpetrate terrible acts of violence or greed in our world becomes one of compassion rather than condemnation.

So to sum up this chapter on the power of love, we need to see that our whole spiritual journey – from our initial awakening to total enlightenment – is all about learning to *be* love and nothing but love. *Being love* equates to an exceptionally high level of consciousness that most human beings have not yet reached, but this does not mean we cannot reach it. In fact, we must attain this awakened state of being, if we are to stand any chance of saving the world for future generations, so that the whole of humankind can eventually evolve into truly loving, compassionate and co-operative beings.

Meditation

The power of love is embracing me.
The power of love is transforming me.

Sit in a meditative position and take several deep breaths to calm your mind.

Imagine a bright star over your crown centre illuminating your whole being in a warm, strong light.

Gently begin to tune into your heart centre at the centre of your chest.

Now imagine your heart centre opening up in the light like the most beautiful flower bud you have ever seen opening its petals layer by layer.

If you find it difficult to open your heart centre, sit quietly and recall a time when you were head over heels in love and allow this beautiful memory to touch your heart.

As your heart centre gently opens in the light, begin to tune into the love energy that is expanding outwards from the core of your being.

Now see, feel or imagine this love energy extending outwards from your open heart to fill every cell of your being.

Rest in love's essence for a while, until your whole being feels suffused with a blissful energy.

Chapter Six

The Power of the Light

If you learn how to build a strong internal bridge to the light through your meditations and other spiritual and energetic practices, you can let the light guide you through your whole life, like a GPS device. Then, if you deviate from the path that the light is mapping out for you, you will feel it in your heart. If, once you have begun to awake, you start to feel stressed out, or in a lot of emotional or physical pain, this is usually a sure sign that you have deviated from the path that the light has marked out for you.

The light will always guide you safely and joyfully along your unique path back home to love. But you do have to sharpen your focus and your consciousness to be able to receive the light's guidance at all times.

Do Not Trust Your Egoic Thought System

Please do not trust your thinking brain to guide you through life. Your brain is part of your egoic existence and so it will always deceive you. Your thinking is all about 'me'. What else? Whenever we move our minds to think, we become self-centred. On the other hand, whenever our individual consciousness soars high enough, we stop thinking and simply dwell in 'I AM', or pure consciousness. But it is very hard for us to dwell in this higher state of mind for any length of time and when our consciousness is low, our brain malfunctions and even hallucinates.

Your brain keeps telling you lies. For example, it will tell you that a former friend, or your ex-partner, has turned into your enemy and therefore you need to defend yourself against them. This is dangerous nonsense!

If you listen to the guidance of your egoic mind, you are doomed. So please refuse to believe your ego's self-righteous opinions and puffed up, crazy beliefs. Your egoic thought system will tell you to hate your loving mother-in-law, or to be terrified of a tiny little spider, or slug. This egoic programming is so deluded! But it will probably take you a huge amount of effort, and many, many 'light episodes', before you see straight through it.

By all means use your brain to perform practical tasks, such as booking a hotel or buying food, but do not let it deceive you about the important things in life. The egoic mind is dysfunctional at best, and at worst, downright vicious, from day one. You think new-born babies are sweet and cuddly? Wait until they scream with rage at you because you have not immediately responded to their needs.

However, you will need to become a long-term, skilled meditator before you will be able to see that all your egoic thoughts, all your likes and dislikes, and all your judgements about the world, other people and yourself are not the slightest bit valid.

Instead of continuing to listen to the crazy logic of the ego, you now urgently need to learn to follow the guidance of the light. The light is the perfect homing device. You may think you are a highly intelligent human being who can find your own way out of the mess you are in. No! Your thinking brain, or lower mind, simply does not have a clue how to guide you home to eternal love and peace.

Your thinking mind is basically deluded, even if you have an IQ of 140+. But your true-self knows the truth beyond all thoughts and beliefs because this self is part of a non-dualistic totality that is all-knowing and all-wise.

There is so much darkness and violence in our world that it now desperately needs pioneering individuals to embody the light very powerfully in order to begin to balance it out. Most human beings are living on a razor's edge, including all world leaders, because they really have no idea how to solve all of the world's endless problems. Basically, they cannot solve world conflicts using the same level of consciousness that created them in the first place.

Fearful egoic consciousness created violent attacks in our world and then our world leaders use the same egoic intelligence to respond with more violence. For example, in response to terrorists waging war on Westerners, Western governments created 'The War against Terrorism'. This will never work.

Normal Thinking is So Confused and Conflicted

The normal human thinking process is not just fearful, it is also extremely confused. This confusion or inner conflict is a core characteristic of our human condition. *'I think, therefore I am,'* should really read, *'I think, therefore I am confused'*. For example, we all tend to think contradictory thoughts such as, 'I want to make a lot of money, but I shouldn't desire loads of money because I am a spiritual person'. 'I must look after my body better, but I just can't resist that doughnut'.

It is as though we all have split minds and therefore split personalities. One part of our personality-self wants one course of action, whilst another part strongly objects to that particular plan for our future happiness. No wonder so many of us are stressed out.

You need to become acutely aware of this core human problem before you can fix it. You need to be exceptionally inquisitive about life to notice how confused and conflicted you are much of the time. As intelligent, well-educated individuals, we usually try to use our human reasoning and logic to make rational, helpful choices in our lives, but we are never truly at peace.

An unawakened human life basically lacks real meaning or purpose. It is just one fleeting experience after another disappearing into nothingness. We all have so many of these dream-like episodes in our lives, without really knowing what any of it means. What is the true meaning of our life? We do not have a clue! But most human beings simply distract themselves from thinking troublesome, but profound, thoughts like this.

Your lower, thinking mind basically knows nothing about life. It certainly cannot predict the future, even though it keeps trying to convince you it knows how to make you happier tomorrow, or next year. Your thinking mind only really knows whether it likes or dislikes something or someone. Everything else is pure guesswork.

Moreover, your intellectual mind can never fully understand another person because it does not truly know them. It constantly makes judgements about them such as, 'He is untrustworthy.' 'She is an angel.' But these are just stories your egoic mind is making up about someone. Even loving parents have to guess what may be best for their children because they do not know. Then their children grow up and complain that their parents made so many wrong choices on their behalf. It takes a tremendous amount of awakening to really see and accept that we do not really know one another or each other's needs at all.

Your thinking mind can only ever try to guess: 'He will make a good husband'. 'She will not be a reliable employee'. Unfortunately, most individuals tend to believe whatever their thoughts are telling them, and so they are slaves to their unreliable beliefs about themselves and others. However, once you begin to awake, you have the perfect opportunity to utilise your connection to the light to transform your personality-self and all its destructive beliefs so that it becomes a real asset on your awakening path, rather than a hindrance.

Re-programming Your Mind

Our soul can awaken spontaneously in an instant. But transforming our personality-self so that it serves our awakened soul can be an extremely painstaking, life-long task. Your soul has only one ultimate purpose down here on earth: to awake and then to serve suffering humanity. But your personality-self can delay your soul fulfilling its true purpose for a very long time. Your personality-self can insist it would rather be rich than awake or world-famous rather than a humble servant of God. But if you allow your personality-self to sabotage your awakening and healing, you will never be truly happy. However rich or famous you may become, you will still feel, deep down at least, very sad indeed!

To awake, you have to cultivate the capacity to rise above all the craziness of your egoic-self and to connect to the light. Only then will you begin to see that you are not just your personality-self. Only then will you notice that your mind is a pre-programmed mind that is now playing tricks on you, like a computer programme that has been corrupted by a really nasty virus.

As young children, we all tend to believe what adults tell us, and so we can be programmed to believe toxic ideas, such as

'All Muslims are a threat to our security,' or 'Christians are our enemies.' Some small children can even be totally brainwashed by abusive adult caretakers into believing that they are inherently 'bad'. One of the most devastating aspects of childhood physical or sexual abuse is that abused children often come to believe they are being punished in some way for their own wickedness. Small children can also be traumatised by isolated events in their childhood, such as one incident of sexual abuse, and these traumatic events then exert a lasting influence over their lives.

Children cannot reject or delete the socialisation they go through during their formative years. But as awakening adults, we have a miraculous chance to look back into our past – with the infinite support and guidance of the light – so that we can delete any old beliefs and stored memories that do not serve our highest good and which could eventually destroy us. We can then replace our self-sabotaging beliefs with new life-affirming convictions that really support life. But understanding the need to do this is not enough to attain mastery of the process. We also need to cultivate a range of skilful means in order to be able to see our own negative programming, delete it, and then replace it with a new life-supporting mindset.

When we believe our own negative, fearful thoughts, we are being hypnotised into thinking we are perishable physical beings. But we are not! We are immortal beings just dreaming that we are mortal.

You and your thinking mind are not the same, whatever Descartes may have said. But you can certainly utilise your thinking mind as a wonderful awakening tool, if you start to question all of your strongly held thoughts and beliefs.

For example, do you believe all of your judgemental thoughts about yourself and others? When you hear a voice in your head telling you that you are so stupid, so unattractive, weak-willed, pathetic, selfish etc., do you instantly believe it or do you question its sanity? When your judgemental mind insists your own mother is unlovable, or your ex is the devil incarnate, do you nod in agreement, or do you tell yourself these are just crazy, unbelievable thoughts?

Until we awake, we all instinctively judge ourselves and others constantly. We think we are making intelligent assessments that will help us to survive and even to thrive in a dangerous world. No! Our negative judgements about everyone and everything are driving us insane, but we just keep doing it, without having a clue about how much we are hurting ourselves and our loved ones.

However, if you raise your consciousness, learn to still your thinking mind for a while each day, and tune into the power of the light, you will gradually rise above the turbulent waters of your lower mind and sharpen your powers of observation. You will finally begin to see the deep, toxic egoic thought system which usually lies hidden from our consciousness. Then you will at least stand a chance of freeing yourself from it.

Without connecting to an internal observer and then illuminating it with a higher light, you will never see the full content of your mind. You will only be aware of a very small percentage of your past-programming. But once you are able to sit and observe yourself with the infinite assistance of a higher light, you will become far less hypnotised by your painful past and toxic beliefs. Most people are basically sleep-walking through life, but your goal from now on should be to walk mindfully along a path illuminated by the light, until you are fully aware of every aspect of your egoic existence.

Advanced Problem Solving

When you are operating at more or less the same consciousness level as the rest of the world, you cannot escape its endless fear and conflict. However, when you rise above this level of consciousness into the light, problems can just seem to disappear as if by magic. If you can bring any problem into an energetic field of love and light, it will just disappear miraculously. This is ultimate problem solving! We can learn to access a much higher intelligence, or light, that can solve any problem that we ask it to solve for us, because a higher power can always transcend any difficulty created by a lower intelligence. But first, we have to know how to rise above our thinking mind which constantly tries to convince us it can solve all our endless problems for us, and yet never delivers the goods.

In our Infinite Tai Chi courses and classes, we encourage students to breathe, rather than to think. We also actively assist them to raise their consciousness above their thinking so that they can open their minds and simply observe their thoughts for a while. Until you begin to quietly observe yourself like this, you can never really know yourself, or solve any of your problems. But when you connect to your inner observer and then illuminate your observer-self with the light, you will finally begin to see the bigger picture.

When you can sit still, calm your fearful, over-busy thinking mind and contemplate in the light, all of your questions are answered, and eventually, miracles can even happen through you. Unfortunately, world leaders do not yet know how to connect to the light. They do not yet contemplate on the world's problems using their non-thinking higher minds, and so the world is basically still a mess.

Normal human existence is so painful because we are all frightened, lonely, loveless, angry and full of egoic pride and self-righteousness. We all feel the pinch of living in a physical world of limitations and disappointments, but miraculously we also all have the free will to commit to transcending all of this by making a conscious choice to bridge the gap between heaven and earth. When we do not have enough light, we all have problems. But when we are fully illuminated by the light, we see that we have no real problems whatsoever.

How to Connect to the Light

'So how' you may well ask, 'can I connect to this mysterious light that will lead me out of my problem-filled life and guide me every step of the way home to eternal love and life'? The simple, but crucial, answer is just to sit still every day, calm your mind, do your very best to open your heart and simply wait until you have an unmistakable experience of the light pouring down on you to illuminate your whole being.

However, even after you become a diligent meditator, you may have to wait patiently for many months, or even years in some cases, before you have an unmistakeable experience of the higher light.

After my own initial spiritual awakening this lifetime, I practised meditating painstakingly for 5-6 years without experiencing anything much happening to me. I certainly did not witness any miracles, and my personality-self remained pretty much the same with all of my neuroses apparently intact. Looking back on that time, I can now see I was being transformed by a higher power, but this transformation took quite some time to become apparent to me.

However, after I had tasted the light just once during my initial awakening, I pursued it obsessively, by meditating with great diligence, until I finally experienced it again. Once you too have tasted the light, you would be crazy not to pursue it with all your might. You cannot pursue the light half-heartedly. You have to commit wholeheartedly to becoming a pioneer in transcending human pain and conflict.

Unfortunately, our unique, subjective experiences of life can never be truly shared. So my telling you that the light is amazing will never totally convince you. You just have to experience it for yourself. Once you do experience the light pouring down on you, you will no longer have to *believe* in a higher power that *might* rescue you from endless suffering: but only if you are deserving enough. You will simply *know* it with the whole of your being, as you feel this higher power supporting you unconditionally.

How does contemplation in the light actually work? First of all, you just need to sit still long enough, and observe your own mind closely enough, to notice just how fearful and self-sabotaging your habitual thoughts actually are.

For example, most people are at least mildly anxious most of the time. Even though your life may be basically OK, if you just sit and quietly tune into your body, you should be able to notice an underlying tension or dis-ease. You never feel 100 per cent safe in this world because you still have a biological survival instinct that constantly prompts your mind to be aware of danger – however remote.

To cope with their underlying anxiety, most people find ways of distracting themselves from it, through for example alcohol or drug use, or an addiction to work, to sex, or even to computer games. But if you stop distracting yourself, and just sit quietly for a while, you will notice you are always at least mildly tense or anxious, even when you can find no specific reason for your anxiety.

I have to tell you the only way out from being imprisoned in more or less constant fear is to awake and then to observe your underlying anxiety, whilst bathing your whole being in a life-supporting light. You will then need to keep up this practice for a long time, until you have observed all the underlying, fear-generating patterns inside your own mind, including all of your anger, hatred, fear and devastation. Only then will you be able to heal yourself by releasing all of this accumulated darkness into the light.

Most people do not dare to sit still, connect to a higher light, and then gaze downwards at their personality-self and all of its programming, because they are not yet brave enough to face all of the stored darkness deep within their own mind. However, I am convinced, after many, many years of seeking a way out of endless fear and anxiety, that only some form of contemplative meditation in the light can reverse our destructive egoic programming.

The egoic thought system is always pushing us to seek without for what we can only find within. We wander around blindly in the dark, looking for a light that is actually hidden deep inside each and every one of us. But please understand that contemplation in the light is not an instant fix. We cannot transcend the ancient, dark, all-embracing egoic thought system overnight. We may well need many years of very diligent contemplative practice, before we can remove all traces of egoic darkness from both our minds and hearts.

Self-Inquiry in the Light

Many busy, highly sophisticated individuals still dismiss meditation as a waste of time because they think of it as sitting still and doing absolutely nothing, and they believe that doing nothing is pointless. But genuine meditation is never blank or empty. In our Infinite Meditations for example, we are learning to calm our lower minds, and then to illuminate our whole being with the light, so we can then utilise this light to lead us on a miraculous journey of self-inquiry and self-transformation.

Meditation is becoming increasingly popular in our modern world as a stress-buster. But meditation is much more than just a trendy technique for calming our over-busy minds and bodies. The core purpose of various ancient and modern forms of meditation is not chilling out, but the discovery, through self-enquiry, of the enlightening truth about ourselves and our lives. So once you make a strong connection to the light, you should contemplate in the light on a very regular basis, until you find out all about the relative truth of our physical existence and then discover the absolute truth of perfect oneness.

Genuine spiritual seekers have tremendous amounts of curiosity about life and so they investigate everything, including their own thoughts and feelings. Buddhist meditators for example do not just de-stress during meditation; they investigate the cause of human suffering and the way out of that suffering.

The Buddha, when he reached a totally enlightened state through his contemplative practices, discovered that his body could be weak, sick, or even dying, but he did not have to suffer because in a totally natural state of mind, there is no suffering, even if the physical body is in pain. Buddha did not say he was creating a new religion. He called his meditative practices 'the science of the mind' and told his followers to transcend all suffering by training their minds to become unattached to all passing phenomena.

But please take note that meditative self-enquiry is different from other types of meditation, such as a mantra meditation, and very different from normal thinking. You might feel confused about meditative self-enquiry in the light for some time, but eventually the essence of this spiritual art will just dawn on you. Meditative contemplation is not thinking. It is as though a blanket of light, or infinite wisdom, illuminates your mind so that you just 'know'. This is a very subtle art. You raise your vibration, connect to the light and then shine the light on yourself, whilst doing your best to think as little as possible, or ideally not to think at all.

Have you ever experienced a time during which you stopped thinking altogether, but knew that you still existed? You do not lose your individual identity just because you stop thinking. You simply become an 'illuminated you' on the mountaintop gazing out onto a vast horizon, rather than a 'lost you' down in the shadowy valley of normal human existence, stumbling about in the gloom, without having a clue where you are going.

When you can clear your mind and dwell in an enlightened, non-thinking state for some time, you will no longer judge the world so much, and you will also be able to tune into real knowing. Through contemplation in the light, you can even become a creative genius. Your brain cells can become much sharper, as they are transformed by the light.

However, sometimes, your consciousness may soar so high and become so expanded that you may forget the name of a friend, or forget to buy the milk that you need for your afternoon tea. So if you still have some kind of worldly life to lead, you cannot bliss yourself out in the light 24/7. You may actually have to lower your consciousness a little from time to time so that you can book an airline ticket or cook a delicious meal for your family.

When we illuminate our minds, we begin to notice the real power of 'Life Itself'. This real power has absolutely no competitiveness, aggression or violence in it. Moreover, when you connect to the higher wisdom of the light, you see everything with much greater clarity. Your awareness naturally expands and so you begin to see the much bigger picture that was previously hidden from your consciousness.

When you 'sit on the mountaintop' bathing your whole being in a higher light, you will have an illuminated, bird's eye view of your life unfolding. You will no longer keep drowning in all of your endless personal problems. At this very high level of consciousness, you can notice, for example, that you have a problem with your job, your relationship, or one of your children. But now, your illuminated mind will not be worrying about any of this, and the perfect action to take will just pop into your mind quite naturally.

Cultivating Compassion for Others

Once you can connect to the light and hold it in your open heart centre and third eye whilst gazing down on the world, you can not only observe all of your own strengths and weaknesses, but also the strengths and weaknesses of others. You will see clearly, but without any egoic judgement, all the unskilled behaviour of those still enslaved by fear and unworthiness. This will enable you to cultivate true understanding and compassion for everyone who is still trapped in their egoic self-centredness, including greedy bankers, abusive partners, violent criminals etc.

As you awake more and more, and your internal observer becomes stronger and much brighter in the light, you may even be able to tune into what other people are thinking and feeling. You will not do this in order to pry into the minds of others, but you will understand them in a much deeper and clearer way than previously. This intuitive understanding will then really enable you to practise the core spiritual art of cultivating compassion for all sentient beings. It will also assist you to forgive others for any unskilled actions on their part that seem to hurt or wound you in some way or another.

Eventually, you will see the bigger picture much more often, and then you will become part of the solution, rather than part of the problem. You will stop being influenced so strongly by your personality-self's moods, negative judgements and projections, and become more and more willing to forgive and let go, so that you become a clear channel for love, light and compassion to extend out into the world around you.

You will spend longer and longer dwelling in inner peace, until your whole life becomes a joy. Please don't go on drifting through life only half alive. Keep illuminating your internal observer, and keep watching your personality-self running its old unhelpful programmes, until you are no longer its slave.

Once we can raise our consciousness to the light, we will no longer be so trapped in physical reality. We will still be careful when crossing the road, but we will no longer totally believe in fearful, physical phenomena. In relationships, we will either communicate the truth or rest in loving silence. We will no longer gossip, talk nonsense, or play childish, egoic games with our loved ones.

When we are not connected to the truth or the light, there is no true communication and we will tend to make a mess, and even end up resenting our loved ones! But when we illuminate our consciousness in the light, we will begin to feel so much inner freedom that we will be able to love others unconditionally, without being needily attached to them.

Connecting to Your Heart-Centred Intuition

Once you know how to connect to the light, you will gain far greater insight into what you should do to fulfil your highest interests and the highest interests of others. This intuition can be experienced like a calling to which you just have to respond.

You may find that you just have to move to another part of the country, or take up a new career, even though your personality-self is perfectly content where you are. Following your heart-centred intuition is not therefore always that convenient or welcome from your personality-self's point of view, but it will undoubtedly assist you to fulfil your soul's highest purpose this lifetime.

True knowing only really starts to dawn into our mind when our third eye and crown centre are fully open, but before this, we can at least try to follow our heart centred intuition, rather than relying on our thinking mind to guide us.

If you have a choice to make about your future, just sit very quietly, feel or imagine your whole being illuminated in a pyramid of bright light, and then ask yourself, 'How does my heart feel about this?' Contemplating on a decision you need to make like this will bring you very different results than if you continue to rely on your thinking mind to tell you what to do. You can ask your illuminated heart what you should do in any difficult situation. Does your heart feel right about a particular course of action? Does it feel joyful and at peace, or troubled?

As you contemplate any decision that you need to make in your life, just ask yourself if your heart sings in relation to the direction you are thinking of taking. For example, you can ask your intuitive heart, 'Should I go and see this person?' or 'Should I visit that country?', and if your heart does not sing at the thought of going: don't go.

Embodying the Light

More and more spiritual seekers are experiencing the light momentarily, but only very advanced practitioners can embody the light and then extend it out into the world around them. You will need to practise a *lot* before you can gain consistency at this level of illumination. Whenever we get totally lost in engaging with the world, we inevitably dim our inner light to some extent, so most spiritual seekers go into higher levels of consciousness and then come back down again for a very long time, before they are consistently dwelling in a heavenly state of consciousness.

When you finally dwell in the light more or less constantly, you will know that the whole physical universe is just an illusion or a magical display. You will be able to look deep within and know you are not really a physical being at all, but a being that is so much greater and brighter.

However, when your consciousness drops and you become more conscious of your physical body, you will be trapped once again, and then you will inevitably experience some fear and anxiety. When our consciousness rises above the physical level, a lot of our fears just disappear. But whenever you are concerned in any way about your physical body, you will feel fearful to some degree or another and then you will struggle.

Fortunately, it is perfectly possible to continue to operate very successfully in a physical body, whilst connecting our consciousness to a much higher level of existence. When we truly know that the physical world is a passing illusion, we are finally liberated from being painfully trapped in physical consciousness. But before you reach this advanced level of awakening, you need to gain consistency in living in love and light.

If you notice that some worldly activities always seem to pull you out of love and light; don't do them. Stressful worldly activities will always drag your mind and your body down to lower vibrational levels. So please refuse to take part in activities that stress you out. Just opt out. Is it really that simple? It certainly can be.

The further you go on the path, the more you will surrender to a much higher power and allow it to guide every aspect of your life. But first, you will need to put a lot of effort into your spiritual practices. You have to know the light intimately before you can surrender into it. Total surrender to the light, or to God, is one of the very last steps on the path because it involves letting your ego die away completely, and you may well not be ready to do this for a long, long time.

However, ultimately, as you merge your little-self completely into the light, your egoic mind will become totally quiet. You will simply know 'I AM', without experiencing any internal dialogue whatsoever. In this blissful, extremely high state of consciousness, you will not want to think, and any thoughts that do pop into your mind will feel like a disturbance or a nuisance.

Holding the Light on Behalf of the Whole of Humanity

We so seldom witness an individual extending nothing but love and light in this world, but your ultimate goal is to extend only God's peace, regardless of what may be happening all around you. You are aiming to shine a light that will be brighter than any star in the firmament. You will not be able to do this next year, nor even – I am guessing here – in several years' time. However, without setting a genuine goal like this, there will be no real transformation or spiritual progress. Eternal peace is literally out of this world, and when you can connect to it constantly, it will simply shine out through you to illuminate the world.

Meanwhile, I ask you from my heart to bless the world unconditionally as often as you possibly can, because the world is collapsing under the weight of our collective fear, hatred and darkness. So we urgently need spiritual practitioners who can balance our troubled world with their illuminated loving intention. We need to practise very diligently, until we can bring light down into a world that is still filled with so much violence and fear.

Many people in this world may be trying to be good and kind, but unless they practise some genuine form of spirituality, they cannot fully anchor the light the world so desperately needs. Good intentions are not enough. Weak, wishy-washy people may sincerely want to save the world, but they have no power whatsoever, and cannot change a thing.

We all have to make every effort to raise our vibration, to evolve to higher states of consciousness, and then to extend peace and light out into the world around us. Every single time we hold a thought of hatred or attack within our minds, we add another spot of darkness to an already very dark, fearful world. So please keep practising until you can extend love and light to all sentient beings and all troubled places and events around the world, day in and day out.

Those of us who are beginning to awake from the insanity of egoic existence urgently need to balance the earth's collective consciousness before humankind self-destructs. This is pioneering work, but every light-filled prayer, meditation, blessing, or smile really does work, because loving energy counterbalances and neutralises fearful energy. When love and light are present, fear is absent, and the forces of darkness just cannot grow any stronger.

Please keep connecting to an eternal reality that lies beyond all illusions. Hold nothing but the absolute truth in your heart and soul and know that you are free. In this truth or this light, everything you may need to fulfil your highest purpose this lifetime will be provided for you. You will simply bathe your whole being in its presence and everything you need to assist your suffering brothers and sisters in this world will manifest miraculously. Mission Impossible completed effortlessly!

Meditation

Divine light descend on me.
Divine light fill me.
Divine light guide me.

Sit quietly and comfortably with a straight spine.

Now use the power of your mind to see, feel, or imagine a very bright light shining down on you like a very bright star.

Gently breathe this bright light down through your seven chakras, illuminating each of your chakras in turn. You may like to bring your palms down to hold the light at each chakra as you do this.

As you bathe your whole being with light, ask the light to answer any question you may have about which direction to take in your life.

Sit quietly for a while. Simply allow all thoughts and feelings to come and go, and whenever your mind wanders off, gently bring it back to contemplating on the infinite wisdom of the light.

At the end of 15-20 minutes, gently open your eyes and write down any insights that occur to you in a notebook that you have left by your side.

Chapter Seven

Awakened Relationships

How many loving relationships have you had since you were born? Did you have a truly loving relationship with your mother and father when you were a child? What about with your siblings? How are your family relationships now? Have you found your soul mate yet? Are you still looking for your 'twin flame'? Are you an incurable romantic at heart, or do you sometimes feel as though close relationships are a minefield of heartache and disappointment?

When our first book, *The Radiant Warrior* was published by Hay House in 2009, Jane and I received a lot of very positive feedback from readers. However, several readers commented that they did not really enjoy the two chapters on relationships because they were so pessimistic. Some readers even thought that I was too cynical about love. However, I can absolutely assure you that this is not the case and to prove it, in this chapter, I am going to suggest how we can create and maintain loving relationships in our lives; but only if we are prepared to put a lot of effort into transcending our inbuilt egoic tendency to sabotage any chance we might otherwise have to find lasting, true love.

This may come as a shock to you, and I am very sorry if I am bursting your romantic bubble, but there is no such thing as a close intimate relationship that is blissful year in and year out, not even if you marry your 'twin flame'. Without awakening, all human relationships are basically substitutes for true love, and we all have hidden egoic agendas in our close personal relationships. These self-centred agendas then block true communication and the exchange of love.

Most people believe that special romantic relationships are based on love, but they are not based on true love at all. The really good news however, is that awakening souls have a wonderful opportunity to transcend their self-centred egoic desires and projections that so often sabotage loving relationships. Awakening individuals thus stand at least a chance of experiencing the bliss of sharing unconditional love with their partner in a 'divine romance'.

Our Egoic Beliefs Sabotage Our Loving Relationships

Everyone down on earth is longing to love and be loved, but most of us are unable to love truly, because we do not feel wholly loveable and so we tend to use others in an attempt to escape from our deep inner loneliness and sense of lack. As you awake and begin to understand the ego or false personality-self, you will see that everyone holds a belief in abandonment, betrayal or imprisonment somewhere deep within their own mind, and these beliefs then seriously harm our ability to form lasting, loving partnerships.

Because subconsciously or even unconsciously, we feel guilty or unworthy, we all tend to sabotage our close relationships. We have all experienced being abandoned, betrayed or imprisoned by our loved ones to some degree or other, although most people fail to see that they also do this to the ones they profess to love. I see a lot of healing clients who tell me all about how they have been abandoned, betrayed or even abused by a parent. Interestingly, none of my clients talk about how they have abandoned or betrayed their parents, yet many, if not most, teenagers emotionally abandon or even betray their parents in one way or another.

Children may seem sweet and innocent when they are very young, but they soon learn how to push their parents' buttons. Married couples too are usually very well matched in a 'pushing each other's buttons contest'. For example, one partner may have a tendency to want to run away from the intimacy of a long-term sexual relationship, whilst the other may have a tendency to cling onto their sexual partner. One partner will play the role of rescuer or persecutor, whilst the other plays the role of victim. Playing egoic games like this in our close relationships seems so normal that most people do not even recognise that they are doing it. Ironically, it is usually quite easy to spot these egoic games in other people's relationships, but much harder to see them clearly in our own relationships.

When we look at other peoples' relationships, we can often spot who is the rescuer or persecutor and who plays the role of victim. We can also see which partner is more likely to abandon the other and which one is more likely to attempt to imprison the other. In this world, we all take it in turns to imprison, abandon, betray, or persecute those closest to us. Some of us do this in very dramatic ways, whilst others of us do it much more subtly, but we all do it to a greater or lesser degree, until we are finally fully healed and fully awake.

If you look bravely and honestly at your past intimate relationships, including your teenage boyfriends or girlfriends, you may well see that you abandoned at least one of your ex-partners, and that at least one of your partners left or abandoned you. You may also see that you played the role of rescuer in one relationship, but adopted the role of victim in another.

You may think to yourself, well that is just how it is; all relationships have their ups and downs. But what you may not realise is that all of our close partnerships, not just our romantic liaisons, are basically temporary alliances based on egoic fear, guilt and lack. As separated egoic-selves, we have an inbuilt tendency to use other people for our own ends and then to dump them when they no longer serve our self-centred egoic agenda. The only way out of the pain this causes us, is for each of us to awake and heal our past wounds and stored grievances about our closest relationships.

In normal life, some people may try to protect themselves from the trauma of being abused or abandoned by someone close to them by drawing up a legal agreement to regulate another's behaviour. For example, more and more people are drawing up pre-nuptial contracts before they get married, particularly if one partner is very rich. But this attempt to regulate human relationships never really works. If we feel enough pain in an intimate relationship, no legal contract will stop us attacking each other or even seeking revenge on one another.

The spiritual way out of this universal mess is the formation of 'conscious partnerships' in which our core intention becomes self-healing and the selfless sharing of unconditional love, rather than that of trying to meet all of our egoic needs through our partner and then blaming them when they cannot fulfil our fantasy of them.

Please consider that the more prepared you are to see and acknowledge your own deep sense of unworthiness, or your belief that you are not wholly loveable, the more you will be able to forgive your partner for all the pain they accidentally cause you or trigger in you. As you awake, the more you will also be ready to heal your own deep sense of not being loveable enough, so that you can then give and receive unconditional love freely and joyfully at all times.

Understanding Karmic Relationships

I will tell you a very familiar story. You meet someone, fall madly in love with them, and then some months, or possibly years later, you find yourself hating them. The person whom you thought you loved so much has now become your worst enemy. Of course, you will think to yourself, 'It's all their fault,' but if you are on your healing journey, you may also start to ask, 'How on earth did this happen? How can true love possibly turn into hate?'

The underlying truth is we usually have a strong karmic connection with our romantic partners. In other words, we have unfinished, unhealed business with them from past lives together. So when you meet someone and feel very attracted to them, or very repelled by them, if you are wise, you will ask your intuitive heart, 'Do I have a karmic connection with this individual that I need to heal?'

Experiencing strong sexual chemistry with someone is often an indication of a karmic connection. If you notice that being with someone leads to a churning in your solar plexus, beware! It is far better to look for a heart-to-heart connection with a potential long-term partner, rather than a very exciting, or even overpowering, sexual chemistry.

Karmic relationships can be horribly sticky and painful. Sometimes, your logical mind will tell you to run away from a potential karmic relationship, and yet you go ahead anyway and then later really regret it. Karmic relationships are based on two egoic-selves coming together in one lifetime, making a mess, and then coming back, lifetime after lifetime, to attack one another again, until one person decides that enough is enough.

If you have a long-standing enmity with another soul that has persisted lifetime after lifetime, you will need a moment of divine grace, or more likely, many moments of grace, to cut through all of your past, painful entanglement. For example, if you have killed someone in a previous life, or been killed by them, you may feel extremely uncomfortable when you meet them again this lifetime, without having a clue why. Similarly, if you have had a powerful romantic connection with someone in a past life, you may well feel a strong attraction to them this lifetime, again without really having a clue about what is going on.

An alternative karmic scenario is that you may feel driven to compensate someone for your unremembered past hurtful behaviour towards them. For example, you may find yourself helping someone out financially without really knowing why you are doing it. If your higher intuition tells you that you are compensating for a past life attack on them, or repaying an unpaid debt from a past-life encounter, you can simply pray for healing and forgiveness to clear this old karmic debt.

As we awake and raise our consciousness, we can actively use all our relationships, including very challenging karmic relationships, primarily for healing purposes, although sometimes, we may have to split from someone physically in order to have enough peace and space to go through this profound healing and forgiveness process.

Sometimes, two souls agree to meet up again this lifetime to do some healing together. These more conscious soul to soul relationships tend to be easier than unawakened karmic relationships, as we consciously commit to forgiving one another. Souls can actually agree to meet up in a particular lifetime and then fight with each other in order to learn the art of true forgiveness. On the other hand, two souls who have cleared all their negative karma together in a past-life may meet up again this lifetime simply to share soul to soul love and companionship, or to work together on a divinely inspired project together that benefits the whole world.

According to ancient Eastern wisdom, we all have karma to clear with other souls who have incarnated alongside of us this lifetime, and sometimes this karma is just so strong it propels us into a disastrous relationship. However, if you know you are clearing karma with your partner, or if you both commit to consciously healing your 'stuff' together, you may find it a lot easier to forgive your partner each time they push your buttons, and thus save a lot of time on your own healing journey back to love.

Self-Healing Can Transform All Our Relationships

Whenever you enter into a conscious partnership, your intention is to see the primary purpose of your relationship as healing your own pre-existing emotional wounds, and extending forgiveness, compassion and unconditional love to your partner. But to begin to do this, you will have to let go of your ego's agenda of trying to grab what little satisfaction it can from other people. You also need to commit to persisting through a challenging process of self-healing and the cultivation of true selflessness in relation to your chosen partner.

Ideally, you should determine the outcome of all your relationships through your initial intention. Please do not get together with anyone with the primary intention of satisfying your own self-centred egoic needs and desires. For example, do not enter into an intimate relationship with the key goal of satisfying your own sexual desires. But of course, most people, when they fall madly in love or lust, will studiously ignore this very helpful suggestion!

There is nothing wrong with enjoying a sexual relationship, but if satisfying your sexual urges becomes your core goal, you are simply trapping yourself in gross, physical consciousness, and this will always cause you to go on suffering. Similarly, if you enter into a close relationship of any kind primarily to assuage your deep down sense of loneliness, it simply will not work. You may well feel blissful for a while when you meet your soul mate, but sooner or later, you will either feel trapped or lonely once again

Some spiritually minded individuals even attempt to barter with God in order to improve their relationship. They promise God that they will forgive their partner for all of their unskilled behaviour, but they are only really prepared to do this as long as their own egoic desires are met. Have you ever prayed like this? I certainly did when I was a young man. For example, you may tell God that you are prepared to overlook your partner's congenital untidiness or lateness, but secretly you are only going to do this, if they will agree to have more regular sex with you.

If you really want to transform an intimate egoic relationship into a truly loving relationship, I am afraid you have to surrender wholeheartedly to God's will. You cannot bargain with the light or with God. You have to pray, and *really* mean, 'Thy will, not mine, be done in this relationship'. Then, and only then, will everything in your relationship fall into place for your highest good and the highest good of your partner – although please note that this will not always please your personality-self!

Joining Together Soul to Soul is So Powerful

If you are on an awakening path, it is usually best to make a conscious choice only to get together with other awakening individuals in intimate relationships. Close relationships are always so challenging, but if both of you are committed to your awakening and healing, both your healing journeys can be quicker, and even fun at times as you laugh together at the insanity of normal life. Joining together soul to soul in an intimate relationship can be so powerful. When a close relationship is not solely based on 'What can I get out of this?' it can become something truly wonderful.

However, if you are going to enter into any close personal relationship, without eventually making a mess, you need to have a very good understanding of human nature and our habitual tendency to blame each other and even to stab each other in the back. You need to be mature enough to understand human beings' instinctive self-centredness and determined enough to vow to do your very best to rise above it.

In order to enjoy lasting harmony with your partner, you also need to know how to extend unconditional love and compassion to them, even whilst their personality-self is driving you to distraction. Can you still love your partner while they are screaming angrily at you, or unfairly accusing you of doing something you have not done? Most human beings cannot do this, but awakened souls can, and please remember that this book has been written for your awakening soul, rather than your personality-self.

Even awakening individuals still have a tendency to indulge in projecting their deep inner pain out onto their partner and then saying or at least thinking to themselves, 'This is all your fault'. But when we become conscious about this, every relationship becomes an opportunity to heal our own pre-existing emotional pain and inner darkness. When you consciously commit to your spiritual path, every challenge, including a very challenging intimate relationship, can be welcomed as a new spiritual adventure, rather than instantly judged a personal disaster.

Practising Loving Communication

If you and your partner are both at least beginning to awake, you will understand that from time to time, both of you will act unskilfully in your relationship, and so you will agree with one another to practise healing, forgiveness, commitment and true communication.

In a conscious partnership, you have to attempt to be emotionally transparent. You have to agree not to hide, suppress, or project your hurt and fear out onto one another. You also need to commit to discussing openly, and respectfully, the issues that arise in your day to day interactions with each other. However, please be aware that only committed spiritual practitioners will be able to do this for any length of time, because we all instinctively try to project our deep belief in our own unworthiness out onto someone else, particularly someone close to us.

In a truly loving, lasting partnership, you will need to be brave enough to reveal all of your true feelings that lurk beneath the surface of your superficial interactions with one another. When you feel a stab of jealousy, or the fear of imprisonment, you will need to share these feelings openly, but considerately, with your partner. However, not so many people in this world are yet brave enough, or skilled enough in 'non-violent communication' to do this.

We all like to hide beneath a thin veneer of 'I'm alright,' 'Everything is fine,' 'I can cope,' even when we are living through the nightmare of a disintegrating love match. We all prefer to keep our vicious thoughts to ourselves and to pretend that they are hurting no-one. But close partners tend to be particularly sensitive to each other's energy and so holding a secret, but hateful thought about your partner without verbalising it, will still have a negative impact on your relationship.

Ask for Higher Help to Transform Your Relationships

As you awake, your suppressed ancient wounds and grievances will sometimes rise up to the surface of your consciousness to be healed. So at times, you are bound to resent your partner and to want to blame them for your unhappiness. But please remember that in a conscious partnership, your intention is true joining, and true healing.

Egos tend to join together as two fragile, separated selves in an attempt to form a defensive, possessive alliance against the rest of the world: 'My husband, 'My wife'. But when two awakening souls join together in love and light, there is an increased opening up to the truth in both of them. Thus, through true joining with another soul, you can usually awake and heal much faster than if you attempt to do this all by yourself.

However, please understand that even when you sincerely commit to a conscious relationship, you cannot actually heal it by using only your own intelligence and effort. You definitely need to rely on the guidance and assistance of a much higher power to stand any chance of transcending the very deeply embodied habit of projection (blaming your partner for *your* pain and *your* deep sense of unworthiness). Normal intimate relationships are a powerful means of hiding from the Truth or from God, and so we always need the infinitely powerful assistance of a much higher power to turn these relationships around from egoic nightmares to spiritual love-fests.

Don't Buy Into Your Partner's Attempts to Guilt Trip You

The ego, particularly an ego that has identified itself as spiritual, may claim that it wants a selfless partnership, but it is actually incapable of making one. The egoic-self is always full of fear, and this fear is magnified if one partner in a relationship begins to awake, heal and grow. If this occurs, the other partner will sense a threat of some kind and may well ask themselves, 'What if they leave me?' They may then even do everything in their power to make the awakening partner feel guilty. For example, they may complain, 'You have spent so much money on going on spiritual retreats. What about that luxury weekend away you promised me?' Or, 'You spend hours meditating every day, and now you are telling me that you do not have any time to come with me to visit my mother. You are so selfish!'

However, when you are spiritually awake and aligned to divine love and light, you simply will not allow yourself to be manipulated by your partner's attempts to guilt trip you like this. Love does not try to overwhelm fear and peace does not fight conflict. It just overlooks it.

But I do have to warn you, if you do not respond to your partner's attempts to guilt trip you, they may try to force you to respond by upping the ante. For example, they may even threaten to leave you, or to take your children from you if you do not go back to behaving 'normally'. This type of emotional blackmail can be extremely uncomfortable, but there is no point in trying to keep the peace by giving into your partner's attempts to guilt trip you and imprison you. It will only keep you both in hell.

Give Your Partner a Break!

All unawakened human beings play egoic games with one another, especially with their sexual partners. So please give your partner a break if they end up betraying your trust in them in some way or another. Moreover, if your partner is not yet awake or healed, they will inevitably try to manipulate you into being the partner they want you to be. But you can never fulfil their inner lack, or match up to their fantasies of who you should be and how you should behave towards them. As you awake, you simply have to do your very best to opt out of all these manipulative egoic games.

Even if your partner becomes very angry with you from time to time, do not accept their projected guilt. Whether or not you stay together physically with a partner who is not yet ready to enter into a conscious relationship is entirely up to you. But whether you stay together or split up, your intention should always remain exactly the same: to extend unconditional love and compassion to your partner, without any egoic expectation of getting something back from them in return.

Awakening Disrupts Our Old Egoic Relationships

If we have read *A Course in Miracles,* we may remember the chapter about turning our 'special relationships' into 'holy relationships', but we will still have no idea what 'holy relationships' really mean, except that they sound spiritual. But if we keep raising our consciousness and begin to awaken to the truth, we will undoubtedly find that all our old egoic relationships are disrupted in some way.

Our egos will then get really pissed off, because we are no longer getting the same sort of personal satisfaction out of our relationships. Please be aware of this. Your personality-self will say to your partner 'Let us have a soul to soul relationship'. But your egoic-self is intrinsically incapable of having a selfless, soul to soul relationship, and when your ego's needs appear not to be met in any relationship, it will simply throw a tantrum. Your ego will always try to use relationships to enhance itself, or to project its inner guilt and fear out onto someone else, and so as you awake, you have to be super-vigilant to rise above all of this.

Please understand that when you give your old egoic relationship to a higher power and genuinely ask for it to become a holy relationship, the shift can be quite dramatic. Your egoic-self will then try desperately to hang on to its old self-centred agenda and so for a while, you may experience *increased* pain and dissatisfaction in your relationship, as your ego tries to sabotage your commitment to awakening and healing.

Your relationship may well seem to get worse before it gets better, as there is now a big gap between what your soul wants to learn from it, and what your ego still wants to get out of it. A lot of people will probably separate at this point, rather than go through all the challenges involved in healing any kind of special relationship.

The problem is that in any close partnership, the more one partner awakes and heals, the more the relationship may seem not to be working out, as its familiar dynamics are turned upside down. So when you change the purpose of your relationship from self-gratification to self-healing, you may well go through a period of time that feels pretty stressful and confusing.

You may experience coldness and indifference towards each other at times, because it will feel to both of you that you no longer share a common purpose. During this period, you need to keep remembering all the good things your partner has done for you and all the love that you have shared with one another. You need to make a big effort to really appreciate your partner's good qualities and to overlook their errors – as you perceive them.

There is nothing much you can do about 'the shit hitting the fan' in a relationship dedicated to your self-healing. You just have to go through this unsettling time in your relationship and realise that neither of you will drop dead. You also need to keep reminding yourself that all of this challenging struggle is part of your healing journey and do as much as you can to keep connecting to the light within. The more you can connect to this light, the less you will be prepared to compromise in your relationship. You will simply say to yourself, 'If my partner is meant to stay with me, they will, and if they are meant to leave me, they will. So be it'.

Rising Above Our Egoic Demands on Those Closest to Us

You will need to cultivate a lot of trust and faith in a much higher all-loving power before you will be strong enough to go through the intense discomfort of healing any intimate relationship. You will need to establish a strong faith that everything will work out perfectly for both for you in the long run, whether you stay together or not. You then have to do your very best not to impose your self-centred agenda onto your partner – for example, 'You should do this because you are my wife.' 'You should not do that because you are my husband'. Can you see how crazy and futile such egoic demands really are?

We can never own another human being or insist they have to sacrifice themselves in some way to meet our egoic needs and demands. Of course, we all do this, but as we awake, we really need to rise above our selfish egoic thoughts and unreasonable demands on others, especially in relation to our partners, our family members and our closest friends and colleagues.

In all of our special relationships, we have a very strong tendency to try and change the other person so that they can fit our fantasy of how we would like them to be. For example, we might insist to ourselves that we cannot be truly happy in our relationship until our partner learns to be tidier, more communicative, more responsive in bed – or whatever! We then try to find ways to push our partner to change. But even if our partner tries to twist themselves into a pretzel to please us, we are still not satisfied.

At its extreme, egoic bullying in close relationships can become abusive. Think for example, of some physically abusive husbands who have justified hitting their wives on the grounds that their dinner was not served on time, or that their wife had returned home late from an office party – two of the many shocking excuses violent men gave for hitting their partners in a PhD on domestic violence that Jane once marked.

So, as much as possible, you should commit to releasing all your expectations of your partner, as these are nearly always selfish and even unreasonable. You and your partner will have so many fantasies about each other that simply cannot be met, no matter how hard you both try to be less demanding in your relationship. In intimate relationships, we will always want the other person to change in some way or another to make us happy, but even if they did so, we still would not be satisfied.

Please Do Not Give Up on Intimate Relationships!

As you begin to see the nasty egoic games we all tend to play with one another in our close relationships, please do not become cold, indifferent, or even cynical about the possibility of finding true love. Keep believing in the miraculous possibility of a true soul to soul romance, and keep committing to healing everything within your own mind and heart that may be currently preventing you from experiencing the bliss of a spiritual romance. Even if you know you are not there yet, keep praying for higher help to transform your relationship into a divinely inspired joining of souls.

I know some wonderfully dedicated and sincere spiritual practitioners who have just given up on intimate relationships in order to concentrate on their own awakening and healing. However, I strongly believe intimate sexual relationships are so intense and 'in your face' that they can offer genuine spiritual practitioners an excellent opportunity for practising the art of letting go, healing our stuff and owning all of our projections – as well as giving us a lot of wonderful shared experiences and happy memories along the way.

So, if you are still relatively young, brave and committed to your healing path, I suggest that you embark on an intimate sexual relationship, if the opportunity comes your way. Not only will such a relationship meet some of your perfectly legitimate physical and emotional needs, but it will also give you a wonderful chance to utilise the potent energy generated by sexual intimacy to fuel the further raising of your consciousness.

It will usually take several years to heal one intimate relationship. It will undoubtedly take you quite some time and effort to see, and then heal, all of your fears about intimacy, as old patterns of manipulation and blaming will keep coming up to the surface to be cleared out of your system.

In any long-term intimate relationship, both partners will attack each other over and over again, and even ridiculously trivial incidents will be enough for one partner to launch a bitter attack on the other. Just a pile of underwear on the bedroom floor, or a delayed meal, can be enough for some couples to launch an all-out war on each other for a while, because they are still blaming each other for their lack of lasting satisfaction within the relationship.

Eventually however, as you awake more and more, you will start to withdraw most of your attack thoughts towards your partner, as you finally master the spiritual art of forgiveness. Your partner will present you with so many opportunities to practise forgiveness, far more than a distant enemy will ever give you. A stranger may stab you in the back once, but your partner will stab you in the back so many times. So your closest relationship can present you with almost countless opportunities to forgive and let go, because you have nowhere to run and nowhere to hide. Perfect!

Sharing Soul to Soul Love with Your Partner

Eventually, as you continue to heal and to awake, your self-centred, 'What about me?' agenda should begin to fade, and then you will realise that you need your partner less and less. Most normal couples try to imprison each other in some way. But if you long for true, lasting love, you have to open the prison door and set each other free. Once, and only once, you have set each other free, can you love each other unconditionally and fearlessly, because you will have finally dissolved so many of the ego's blocks to sharing true love.

At this stage, your projection of pain and blame onto your partner should really begin to lessen. You may still blame them from time to time, but this blaming will become more subtle, and you will enjoy more and more soul appreciation of your partner's beautiful essence, especially when you have experienced many precious moments of sharing true love with one another.

Even non-awakening couples usually experience occasional moments of pure love in their relationship, for example when they are making love in complete synch with one another, or when they share the miraculous moment of the birth of their first child. But their mutual unhealed grievances then tend to pile up and make them forget these shared moments of true love. However, in a committed long-term conscious partnership, you need to choose to remember these times of pure love and appreciation for your partner. You also need to relinquish all your old egoic goals and grievances over and over again, until you do not need to cling possessively to your partner, or to blame them for your pain or dissatisfaction with life anymore.

Eventually, you should be able to love your partner soul to soul, rather than unhealed personality-self to unhealed personality-self. This is so liberating because soul love never dies. Personalities in bodies are really just dream figures that come and go very quickly. But if you love someone soul to soul, you can still be at peace and in love, even when they leave their body, although you may still grieve the loss of their physical presence in your life for quite some time.

Moreover, when your special relationship is fully healed, the love that you will share with one another will simply extend out naturally into the world around you. You will open wide the doors of your two beautifully connected hearts and let everyone in to share the pure and powerful love that you and your partner are now mutually sharing, increasing and extending.

The Lasting Joy of a Divine Romance

If, after reading all this, you still want to commit to a long term, intimate relationship, please do your very best to find a partner with whom you can share unconditional love. Unfortunately, you cannot just decide to go out into the world and find a 'divine romance partner'. There is, as yet, no enlightened dating agency that will match you up with a completely awakened and healed soul-partner.

If you truly long for a soul to soul romance, you should focus primarily on healing your own insecurities, layer after layer, until you re-connect to your heart's pure intention. Like attracts like, and so you can only attract a partner capable of sharing true love, if your intentions are pure and loving. Moreover, before you can truly love another human being for any length of time, you have to be able to love yourself unconditionally, and this takes some practice!

Before you can experience the bliss of a divine romance, you also need to be in love with all of life. In a divine romance, you are not really making love to just one other human being. You are making love to the divinity in that person and this same divinity is in each and every one of us.

If you are already in a long-term relationship, please do your best to understand that you can never insist that your partner gives up their unrealistic expectations of you or push them to change and become less needily attached to you. Your partner may choose to heal their insecurities as you heal yours, or they may not. We can never push anyone else to change one iota. We can only commit, one hundred per cent, to healing ourselves, when we have totally transcended our egoic relationships, with all their aggressiveness, possessiveness, jealousy, rage, anxiety, projected guilt and self-hatred. However, if we are exceptionally blessed this lifetime, we may meet another awakening individual, and both of us may then eventually experience the joy of sharing a divine romance for a while.

In a divine romance, two individuals join together to bathe in God's infinite love as one, unified child of God. When we finally reach this extremely advanced level of human evolution, we will no longer try to cling to another body to ward off loneliness or sexual frustration. We will just be an open field of loving energy. We will no longer desperately try to merge with another body to compensate for our lack of inner wholeness. We will come together as two healed and whole souls longing to merge into pure, effortless oneness.

This is what we all really want, deep in our hearts. We all long to return home to our natural wholeness. We long to be truly alive, and completely connected to one another, with absolutely no separation between us. We are desperate to know that we are loveable and to experience ourselves as a drop of love totally merged into an infinite ocean of love.

Establishing a divine romance between you and your partner can definitely be one beautiful way of connecting to the ocean of love that holds us all blissfully within itself. So please, do not give up on close loving relationships just because the going may seem to get rough from time to time. Honour the longing deep in your heart to find true love and to then share it with others, and do not stop searching for that love until it fills you to overflowing. Then simply share this love with everyone you meet, including, if you are so inclined, your chosen soul mate this lifetime.

Meditation

Today I give heartfelt thanks to my partner and my ex-partners for all the love and kindness that they have shared with me.

Sit quietly in a meditative position and connect to a bright star above your crown centre that then bathes you in a very bright light.

Now breathe this awakening light gently in and out of your heart centre and imagine it opening like a beautiful flower unfolding its petals in bright sunlight.

Bring your current partner, or an ex-partner, into your mind and gently recall all the wonderful moments you have shared together.

Recall all the loving things your partner, or ex-partner, has done for you and send them heartfelt thanks for each beautiful memory.

Fill your heart with love, and then extend this love to your partner and ex-partners through your open heart.

If you find this meditation difficult to do, think of someone whom you love, fill your heart with gratitude for their presence in your life and then gently extend that loving energy to your partner or to your ex.

Chapter Eight
Awakened Sexuality

We Both Glorify and Condemn Sex

Sex is always an exciting subject, but most of us find it difficult to talk about openly, even with our sexual partner. There is so much confusion in all our minds about sex. I was both fascinated and so confused about sex when I was young, and nobody seemed to be able to clarify this incredibly important subject for me. But I now know that sexual energy can be turned into rocket fuel to blast us up to higher levels of consciousness. I know that we can ultimately utilise this natural, but often problematic energy on our awakening journey by transforming it into pure spiritual gold

Even if you do not currently have a sexual partner, or wish to remain celibate for the rest of your life, you can still cultivate and purify your sexual energy and then use it to enhance your health, your vitality and your creativity. But first, you need to gain some understanding about why sex can be such a problem in so many of our lives.

Our society both glorifies and condemns sexual activity, and we all tend to be a little embarrassed about sexual matters. I have never met anyone who was completely immune to the challenges posed by human sexuality and sexual behaviour. There is a lot of human unhappiness related to sex, and we all tend to have at least some shame and guilt about sex somewhere in our minds. But none of us really want to look at this too closely.

Sexual energy seems to cause many problems in our society. Some very disturbed individuals may even commit murder in a desperate attempt to satisfy their sexual cravings, or as a revenge attack for perceived sexual rejection of some kind. Many individuals have also been victims of sexual violence.

It is now estimated, for example, that approximately one in four women worldwide will experience some form of sexual violence during their lifetime. Some individuals definitely use sex as a weapon. Rape is a very big problem for women the world over, but some women can also use sex as a weapon, for example, by withholding sex to punish their partner.

Even in normal, non-abusive sexual relationships, there are still so many painful traps that we tend to fall into over and over again. For example, sexual desire seems to fade in almost all long-term sexual relationships and then society tells us we are missing out and that we need to re-ignite our sexual fire, even if we are in our 70s.

The good news however, is that if you begin to gain some understanding about the darker side of human sexuality, particularly the dynamics of what I will call 'getting' and 'performing' in relation to sex, you can then begin to transcend these lower levels of sexual consciousness and even utilise your sexual energy for a much higher purpose. If you are determined to do so, you can learn how to harness sexual energy to cultivate a genuine passion for life that will sustain you through all kinds of worldly challenges and disappointments.

Do You Know How to Manage Your Sexual Energy?

Really high powered, extremely successful individuals often seem to have exceptional levels of sexual energy and charisma.

As an energy practitioner, I have noticed that certain presidents of the United States, some high level European politicians, many top business men and women, plus of course, film stars and sport stars have a lot of sexual energy.

However, I have also observed that most people, including many highly intelligent and successful individuals, just do not know how to manage their sexual energy successfully. If you do not know how to handle sexual energy, it can really destabilise you and cause you tremendous amounts of pain and suffering. On the other hand, if you learn to utilise your sexual energy effectively, it can be a wonderful asset to you in this world, even if you are now primarily committed to your spiritual awakening.

As you begin to rise above the darker levels of sexuality into the sunlight of 'loving sex', you can not only have more fulfilling and less painful sexual relationships, you can also utilise your purified sexual energy to empower yourself. According to ancient Taoist wisdom, if you combine positive sexual energy with the power of nature, the world is your oyster! As you heal and purify your sexual energy, and learn how to cultivate and then conserve it, you should find that you have much greater focus, drive and vitality than before. You may even begin to notice that other people seem to find you charismatic and inspiring, which in turn will assist you to succeed in all types of worldly endeavours.

If your main priority in life is now your awakening, please do not ignore the subject of sex on the grounds that it is 'not spiritual'. You probably still have some important lessons to learn about managing your sexual energy. For example, as you commit to your spiritual journey, you may well experience some conflict over any continuing sexual desires and fantasies, particularly if you are still young and healthy.

You may also believe, on some level or another, that the spiritual path is about sacrifice, and you will possibly think that if you are spiritual, it is wrong to still want to be sexually attractive, or to have a great sex life. If despite this belief, you keep on experiencing a load of sexual energy and desires, you may even have a tendency to beat yourself up for not being a purer spiritual practitioner.

Many human physical and material desires, including sexual ones, do tend to be filled with conflict, fear and underlying guilt, and thus cause us a lot of stress, dissatisfaction and unhappiness. But rather than suppressing these desires, on the grounds that they are not spiritual, I strongly believe that it is best to purify them by healing our guilt around them once and for all.

To begin to transcend all of your guilt and confusion around sex, you first need to understand that you do not have to sacrifice your sexual desires in order to be spiritual. You just have to rise above any gross energy and consciousness that may be attached to them. So for example, if a sexual fantasy appears in your mind whilst you are meditating, please don't try to suppress it, or you will simply create further conflict and separation within your own mind. Once you are in touch with the observer within your own mind, you can watch sexual fantasies appearing in your mind, pull your mind back over and over from getting lost in them, and then bathe them in spiritual light to purify them.

Sexual Energy is Neither Good nor Bad

Let us continue our exploration of this highly controversial topic with a crucial fact: human sexuality is a totally natural and essential energy. Without sexual energy, there would be no life on earth. But you do have to ask yourself, 'What am I going to use this natural energy for? Am I going to use my sexual energy to try to fulfil my physical desires – as the vast majority of human beings do? Or am I going to use my sexual energy primarily as super-fuel for my spiritual journey?'

Only a handful of human beings out of 7 billion of us are currently using their sexual energy primarily to fulfil a spiritual purpose. But however difficult or complicated it may be, I do believe that it is possible to use sexual energy as fuel for enlightenment. As Kenneth Wapnick pointed out, the key issue is never whether we should or should not do something in this illusory world. So the question is not really 'Should I have a sexual relationship or not?' The real question to ask is whether or not we can make love to someone without guilt and without accidentally inflicting any further pain or suffering on anyone, including ourselves.

If you are sexually active, please try not to worry about your sex life too much. Try to be more natural and less guilt ridden about it. Guilt has a very low vibration, and there is so much guilt associated with sex in our culture, it is not surprising to me that we have very high rates of sexual problems in our society.

Some people feel ashamed in relation to their sexuality or past sexual activity, and shame has an even lower vibration than guilt. Sexual energy itself has neither a positive nor a negative effect on the level of our consciousness, but if you add guilt and shame to it, your consciousness can sink right down to a very low, gross level. On the other hand, if you purify your sexual energy, it can actually create a very high, strong vibration in your system that can assist you to raise your consciousness to the level of unconditional love and beyond.

Our whole society makes such a drama out of sex and so-called sexual misconduct, but sex is one of the most natural activities in the world. The birds and the bees don't say to themselves, 'Should we do it or not do it?' But we humans always have to complicate everything with our dramatic stories, our fears and phobias, our fantasies and desires, our greed and our underlying subconscious feelings of guilt, shame and unworthiness. Our deep sense of unworthiness is ultimately the core issue we all need to heal, and this really has nothing to do with whether we are sexually active or celibate.

So, if you currently engage in sexual acts in order to give physical and emotional pleasure to your partner and yourself, please note that there is absolutely nothing wrong with this. Just do your best to be an unselfish lover and to cultivate genuine love and gratitude for your sexual partner. Whenever you make love, try not to make love selfishly. Make your partner's satisfaction your primary concern and cultivate loving feelings for your partner so that you can create a harmonious sexual energy together.

Understanding Sexual Desire

Sexual desire is such a vast subject. For example have you ever wondered where sexual desire comes from? Scientists will tell you that it is just a biological urge, but I have to tell you that from a spiritual perspective, our sexual desires stem from an inner feeling of lack. Out of our egoic separation from oneness or totality, we all have a deep sense of not being whole, and then from a very early age, most human beings strongly identify themselves as being either male or female. At the same time, we feel that we lack something. If we are a boy, we cannot be a girl, and vice versa.

Then when we hit adolescence, the sexual hormones kick in and all hell tends to break loose. Now we really start to long for our 'other half'. Gay individuals tend to look for a feminine or masculine other half in the same way as straight individuals do.

As physical beings living in a world of duality, we never feel truly whole. Some of us are more energetically yin and some of us are more yang, but none of us are a combination of yin and yang in perfect balance and harmony. So many individuals tell me that they long to meet their soul mate, but if you desperately want a man, I would suggest to you that you probably lack male energy in your own system. If you long for a woman or an effeminate man to become your other half, you probably lack internal female energy.

Obsessive sexual desires fundamentally arise because we do not feel complete or whole, but sexual desires also tend to have a lot of fire energy associated with them. Most of us have experienced this fiery energy rising up in our system, especially during our teenage years and early 20s. Sexual desire can become an extremely strong, burning desire that at times may even seem to consume us. When we are in thrall to this fiery energy, our desire for a man or a woman can rage so strongly that we can become convinced that only by finding a sexual partner can we feel whole, or satisfied.

You can want a man or a woman so much that you completely lose your centre and become mentally, emotionally and energetically unbalanced. All your energy goes outwards in an attempt to attract a sexual partner. Your reason just cannot help you when you feel like this, and no one can tell you that the object of your desire is not the right one for you. Your best friend may warn you that the object of your burning desire is an absolute nightmare, and yet you will not hear a word said against him or her.

When we began to feel strong sexual desire in our early or mid-teens, we probably felt pretty confused because on the one hand, we saw sexual images everywhere, for example on advertising hoardings, and on the other hand, we were being told not to do it. Even today, in our sexually permissive Western society, many young women are still warned about the dangers of sexual activity and urged not to risk becoming pregnant, or warned that they will be labelled a 'slut' if they have too many sexual partners. Young men on the other hand may feel guilty, or even ashamed, as they access the porn sites that are now all over the internet.

A lot of teenagers turn to masturbation to release all the pent up fiery sexual energy within them, but masturbation does not remove the psychological yearning for the opposite sex. The craving is still there, combined with feelings of guilt and shame, and all this gives most young people a really hard time. Some young people, trainee Catholic priests for example, may try very hard to suppress all their sexual desires, but usually this only works to a degree, because in most young people, sexual desire is a very powerful force indeed.

Problematic Sexual Energy

Some individuals eventually choose to suppress their sexual energy because of feelings of shame or repulsion. Many traditional religions still teach that the sexual act is, in many circumstances, a sin. Moreover, any experience of sexual abuse in childhood (and many, many children have such experiences) can lead to a child feeling deep shame and even self-loathing that can later manifest as a fear of sex, or even a phobic dislike of sexual intercourse. This negative low sexual energy is very different from someone who may naturally have a low sex drive, because, for example, they do not have a lot of testosterone or oestrogen in their system.

If we suppress or try to suppress, our natural sexual drive, we may become energetically depressed or depleted, and this in turn can lead to long-lasting emotional problems, such as chronic depression or anxiety. Even those who enjoy the sexual act can sometimes feel a depletion of energy after an orgasm, and then they can temporarily experience a sense of lethargy, anxiety, or even guilt and shame.

On the other hand, some individuals with a lot of fiery but dark sexual energy can become aggressive sexually, as they project their own deep self-hatred outwards onto their sexual partner or partners. Unfortunately, unhealed individuals can only do two things with all their inner darkness and self-hatred around sex. They can either try to suppress it, or they can try to project it outwards onto others.

Some individuals may even end up feeling an aversion for their sexual partner, particularly when the initial fiery desire for them dies down because they are so disappointed that their partner has totally failed to live up to their unrealistic fantasy of them. Some disillusioned sexual partners tragically end up waging war against each other, or at least engaging in a cold war in which they hardly ever speak to each other, or show each other any real affection.

High sexual energy can sometimes be associated with a lot of anger and frustration. We have all seen men who become quite aggressive when a woman flirts with them sexually and then rejects their advances, and sometimes this aggression can even lead to violence.

Sexual frustration can lead to sexual anger that in extreme cases may even lead to a sexual assault of some kind. Rape is linked to some human beings' accumulated inner darkness and deep sense of self-loathing. It is also related to some men's need to control others in a vain attempt to boost their own self-esteem. In civilised societies, most of us try to control others in a relatively civilised way, but sometimes our baser instincts flare up, particularly in an individual with a very low level of consciousness, and then all hell can break loose. In our society, many of us learn to play quite sophisticated sexual games with one another, but sometimes, these games can turn extremely nasty.

There can also be a lot of egoic pride attached to high levels of sexual energy. Just think of men's magazines in which young men display their six packs to prove that they are sexually attractive, strong and potent. We also have female models displaying their sexuality in glossy women's magazines, and all these sexual images feed our sexual desires and fantasies, before we even explore the much murkier world of pornography. If someone believes that they are 'good in bed', they can become rather arrogant about their sexual prowess and this arrogance can lead them to indulge in hurtful sexual behaviour, or even to belittle sexual partners, or potential partners, who do not live up to their 'high sexual standards'.

Confusing Sexual Desire with Love

Sexual desire and true love are very different energetically and emotionally, but we all tend to confuse sexual desire and love, particularly when we are young and full of sexual longing. We think that desperately wanting someone must mean we love them, but this is often a big mistake. Sexual desire is very often based on our sense of lack, not love. When we desperately long for the object of our sexual desire to come closer to us, we are actually projecting our inner search for wholeness out into the external world. We are desperately looking for love in all the wrong places.

The equation is: the more you desperately want and need someone, the more you believe – whether consciously or not – that you are not whole; that you lack something only another person can give you. Ironically, once you then meet this person and believe your lack has been filled, you will tend to experience a drop in sexual desire, which is one reason why women complain that men just fall asleep straight after orgasm.

If someone you desire rejects you, you feel so sad and lonely, but if they reciprocate your advances and you stay locked together with them for say 72 hours non-stop, you may well find yourself longing for a break from them. You will say, 'I love you so much, but I just need my own space right now'. If your loved one needily sticks to you like glue for any length of time, you will get pretty fed up. I can more or less guarantee it. You will inevitably start to push your partner away because all your desire for them will have disappeared, as you get more closeness than you bargained for.

Becoming Addicted to Being Sexually Attractive

Sexual desire can very easily become an addiction. When they haven't got a sexual partner, some human beings will do virtually anything to get sexual satisfaction. Some individuals pursue others for sex very clumsily, others do it much more subtly, but most of us do it one way or another. In our culture, most of us try so hard to become sexually desirable. Women spend a fortune on diets, face creams, make-up, perfumes etc., whilst some men even spend thousands and thousands of pounds on a fancy, fast car to lure an attractive member of the opposite sex into their life.

My sincere advice to you is this: if someone is really desperate to get you into bed, run away, because they will inevitably be a pretty neurotic, unhealed individual. Moreover, try not to get into a relationship with someone who is obsessed by their sexual attractiveness, because again they are deep down unhealed and unbalanced. They are trying to boost their self-esteem by being exceptionally sexually attractive, or outstandingly good in bed. But if they do not deliver a brilliant sexual performance, they can very easily become deflated or even depressed. Underneath the glossy exterior of a man with the perfect six-pack, or a woman with perfect, silicone filled breasts, you will often find an individual with low self-esteem, and such individuals can be walking time bombs.

There is nothing wrong with wanting to have a fit and attractive body, but some people can become addicted to making their physical body more and more sexually attractive. They can become a slave to their addiction to looking 'sexy'. In fact, many of us, at some time in our lives, have been at least a little addicted to looking sexually attractive. We have also experienced the pain of not being able to live up to the unreachable standards of sexual attractiveness set by Hollywood and the mass media. We know that all the models in the glossy magazines have been airbrushed into perfection, but we may still want to look like them, even when we reach the age when grey hair and wrinkles are inevitable.

Many of us even become permanently stuck in a 'getting' mentality in relation to sexual relationships. For example, some women may say to themselves, 'If only I could lose a few pounds, I could then get a George Clooney look-alike, and live happily ever after.' Men may tell themselves, 'Tonight, I will finally get lucky and score a really hot date who looks just like Jennifer Lopez.' These are actually insane fantasies, but they are so common that we hardly notice how crazy they are.

A getting mentality in relation to sex has a relatively low energetic vibration, and so even quite advanced spiritual practitioners can find that their level of consciousness actually drops when they fall in love and go all out to attract the object of their desire. I have seen this happen to several of my most promising young students, but what can I do? The fantasy of falling in love and living happily ever after is far too powerful for me to persuade anyone in its grip that it is just a form of temporary insanity.

Whenever we long to physically connect to another's body, we are actually treating the other person as an object, and if we observe ourselves closely enough when we do this, we will find some emotional pain underneath our desire. When someone longs for us to become their sexual partner, we may feel temporarily boosted by their attention, but eventually all special desire like this tends to fade. Whenever we get the object we long for, sooner or later, we become relatively indifferent to it. A physical desire fulfilled does not therefore lead to lasting satisfaction; it usually leads to yet another physical desire.

Just think about this for a minute or two. If you long for chocolate, and then fulfil your desire by eating a huge bar of chocolate all in one go, you will probably no longer desire any chocolate for a while. But some time later, you may well develop a new craving for crisps or nuts. Fulfilling our sexual desires tends to work in a similar way. This is one reason why the most intense love affair can quite quickly turn sour, and why, when society allows it, many individuals pursue one sexual partner after another or even more than one sexual partner at the same time.

Just as we can overdose on one type of food like chocolate, we can overdose on one sexual partner. I am sorry to have to shatter your romantic illusions, but Romeo and Juliet only became symbols of everlasting love because they both died before they could get terminally bored with one another. Of course, we all like to believe that if only we could possess the object of our desire, we would find lasting fulfilment. But our own experiences, time after time, tell us that this wonderful romantic fantasy is just an illusion.

Putting on a Sexual Performance

When we think that we lack something, we are usually prepared to go through hoops in order to get it, and when we are trying to attract and keep a sexual partner, we all tend to put on a big performance. Putting on a sexual performance can even seem so romantic. We all have beautiful sexual fantasies in our heads, a lot of them based on Hollywood films or romantic novels, or a combination of the two. Remember, for example, Darcy (Colin Firth) in the classic 1995 TV adaptation of Pride and Prejudice coming out of the lake in that wet shirt to surprise Elizabeth Bennet? (Jane's favourite romantic fantasy, not mine!!).

When we are in a performance mentality in relation to sex, we all try to perform to the very best of our ability. We try to please our partner and ourselves through a fantastic sexual performance. Men try to prolong their erection, while women, so I have been told, have even been known to fake orgasms to give a really impressive sexual performance. Of course, the modern media's emphasis on peak sexual performances, and multiple, simultaneous orgasms, puts us under a lot of pressure to perform in bed, and therefore adds to our stress around our sexual performances.

There is now so much pressure on both men and women to perform sexually. Mainstream medicine offers Viagra for older men and hormone replacement therapy for older women, whilst more adventurous souls can go on Tantric Sex workshops, or practise the exercises from books such as Mantak Chia's *The Multi-Orgasmic Couple*. The problem is: what if you cannot perform? No one can give peak sexual performances night after night, and month after month, without wilting or burning out, sooner or later. One night, you may perform so well sexually, but the next night, the performance falls flat, and you end up feeling disappointed, worried or even depressed.

Unfortunately, the putting in a top performance approach to sexual intercourse does not work in the long run. It does not bring the lasting satisfaction and pleasure that so many of us are seeking. There is now a billion dollar industry giving us all sorts of advice and even mechanical and electrical aids, to enhance our sexual performance. But there is still so much pain, dissatisfaction and disappointment in this performing approach to sexuality that we really need to begin to ask ourselves, 'What on earth are we all doing wrong, and how can we finally get it right?

Forgiving Ourselves and All Our Sexual Partners

To transcend all the confusion, guilt and emotional pain associated with our sexual desires, we need to start by adopting a loving, compassionate approach towards all our sexual partners, sexual preferences, sexual problems and sexual disappointments. We need to focus on healing all our past mistakes and grievances in relation to sex, including all the guilt, pain or resentment attached to them. We really have to forgive all our past sexual partners, even the most fleeting ones, one by one. We need to forgive them for all the pain and hurt they seemed to cause us, and then forgive ourselves for any pain that we may have accidentally inflicted on them.

Eventually, we have to be ready to send unconditional love and total forgiveness to all of our sexual partners. If we are really determined to free ourselves from all sexually related hurt, disappointment and guilt, we also need to cultivate genuine compassion for all our sexual partners, past and present, however badly we think they may have treated us. If we do not forgive ourselves and all our sexual partners for all the hurt we have imposed on one another, we will still be walking time bombs just waiting to explode with rage at the next sexual disappointment, attack, betrayal or abandonment.

As we awake from the nightmare of unhealed human relationships, including unhealed sexual relationships, we need to start to let go and forgive all past hurts, including all those very powerfully painful memories of sexual attacks or rebuffs.

To be able do this, we have to open our heart to true love, even if that means really feeling all the past pain that we have experienced in relation to our most intimate relationships. We need to open our hearts, so that we can become more genuinely loving, compassionate and understanding about all sexual issues. Until we are fully healed and awake, we all tend to make mistakes in relation to our sexual energy and desires, and these mistakes can really hurt us and anyone involved with us. But as we open our hearts and connect to an unconditional love way beyond human neediness and desire, we can begin to release all of this heartache layer after layer, until only true love remains.

When you can simply sit still in meditation, raise your consciousness, open your heart and experience unconditional love pouring through you, you will no longer have such a strong need to go out and try to attach yourself to another human being in a futile attempt to fill up your inner lack. You will be able to admire a beautiful woman, or a handsome man, passing you by in the street without having the thought, 'I wish I could get your phone number,' or even, 'I wish I could get you into bed.'

When you feel more whole within yourself, you will not feel such a desperate need to go out to find a sexual partner. You will be able to appreciate a beautiful body, or a warm, friendly personality, without needing to grab hold of it and make it yours.

The more you find true love, light, peace and joy deep within you, the more all of your desires for external pleasure or satisfaction will eventually begin to die down, including all of your self-centred sexual desires. You will become less needily attached to people in the external world, including your sexual partner. You will stop objectifying your partner so much, and stop unconsciously exchanging so much guilt with them. Furthermore, you will finally be able to utilise your sexual energy as fuel for your awakening. This is all wonderfully liberating! So please do not rest on your laurels until you reach this very advanced point in your healing journey.

Once you are finally free from the pain of needy, egoic attachments, if your sexual partner decides that he or she wants to leave you, you may well feel shocked or extremely sad for a while, but you will not feel devastated, and you will still extend unconditional love to them even as they are leaving you. But of course, you will need to be an extremely advanced spiritual practitioner to maintain this level of equanimity in the face of a big worldly blow to your self-esteem and emotional security.

Everytime that you are sexually intimate with someone, I am afraid that you can expect some stored emotional hurt or grievance to rise up to be released. But the more you commit to purifying your sexual energy and desires, and to bringing true love into your love making, the more sexual healing will happen quite naturally.

Spiritual Love Making

Once we have released and healed a lot of our stored pain around sex and sexual relationships, we can finally choose to have a sexual partnership based on sharing love, rather than one based on needy attachment, or sexual addiction. One beautiful way to share genuine love with your sexual partner is to just sit quietly, directly opposite them, open your heart, tune into unconditional love, and then gently extend love energy to your partner who, ideally, is doing the same thing to you.

In this intimate exercise, neither of you are trying to get anything from each other, nor are you trying to impress each other in any way. You simply raise your vibration, if possible to the level of unconditional love, and then connect to each other without any self-centred expectations. You then extend love to each other in a state of pure peace and harmony.

Once you have established this loving exchange, you can, if you wish, begin to make love to each other physically, but your primary goal is not to gain sensual pleasure from being sexually intimate with your partner. Your core intention is purely to share love with them, heart to heart and soul to soul. As you do this, you can even melt into each other energetically and experience the bliss of true union. But the emphasis in this awakened type of love making is not on physical or emotional sensations; your main goal is to make love soul to soul beyond all physical form.

Although this form of love making is not about technique, if you are a man, you will probably need to practise being able to hold an erection, whilst still being open to your partner energetically and emotionally. In spiritual love-making, the man needs to be able to make love with his body, without drowning in his physical sensations, and without being over-stimulated to ejaculate too soon and thus lose his heart to heart connection with his partner. A man may even need to do something like counting his breaths in order to bridge the gap between his fiery sexual energy and this open-hearted melting into union with his beloved.

Because women's sexual energy and orgasm are more internal than men's, men usually have to make more of an effort to transcend the purely physical aspects of the sexual act. It can take a lot of disciplined mind training, and even some strengthening of certain muscles, for a man to overcome the natural tendency to ejaculate outwards at a certain point in love making. If a man drinks too much alcohol before making love, it will be much harder for him to control his ejaculation. In fact, I highly recommend that if you do wish to practise spiritual love making, you should drink very little alcohol or none at all, before you begin, so that your energy remains pure and your mind remains clear and focussed.

It is certainly well worth a man making every effort to control his ejaculation during love-making, because he can then use the amazing sexual energy generated by prolonged love-making to cocoon his body and his partner's body in a truly empowering and loving field of energy. This will revolutionise the sexual act.

When you can really open your heart to your partner as you make love to them, the connection between you can go really deep. You can make love to one another with the intention of true soul to soul joining and expansion, rather than trying to fill up your inner sense of lack. This soul to soul joining will then in turn lead to a much deeper appreciation of the divine qualities of your sexual partner's soul and so two awakened partners can even enjoy a 'divine romance'.

Please understand that unless your love making has true freedom, beauty, compassion, caring and understanding in it, it is basically just an expression of our basic drive to re-create. If the sexual act has no love in it, it is really not much higher in terms of consciousness than sex between animals. If you just focus on gaining sensual bodily pleasure from the sexual act, you can very easily get hooked on sex as a physical high, rather than choosing to turn love-making into an integral part of a divine romance.

In spiritual love making, you are aiming for divine union, not sensual pleasure. You are not really making love to the body or the personality of your partner. You are connecting to their essence or soul. You are fully present when you make love and in this high state of consciousness, you see the god or goddess in each other as you cultivate love energy together. Taoist practitioners call this 'dual cultivation'. When two advanced practitioners practice dual cultivation, the love energy that they can generate together can be so expansive that they can use it to raise their vibration and consciousness to an exceptionally high level. Now, instead of just having sex, they are practising spiritual love making.

In spiritual love making, two souls melt together into supreme oneness. You no longer focus on two bodies intermingling, but on two souls melting into the ultimate. Sex is not just sex anymore. It is a divine merging or an angelic dancing together in the light. The divine bliss of two souls joining in the light like this is eternal and will stay with you. Physical orgasms, in contrast, are very short lived and soon forgotten, except for a vague memeory or an egoic need to repeat a physically pleasurable experience.

When you master the art of spiritual love making by purifying your sexual energy and by rising above physical pleasure seeking, the sexual act can finally become one of the most beautiful acts on earth.

At the most advanced level of Taoist practice, the sexual act becomes a high state of energy expansion and fusion, in which you make love as divine feminine and divine masculine energies coming together in perfect harmony. As these energies fuse together in sexual union, you and your partner can both merge into a wholeness that lies beyond all physical form. Orgasmic energy is now converted into a very powerful inner light. As you dwell together in this light, you can both experience wave after wave of internal bliss, as you both become totally infused with radiant internal chi.

Now the sexual act has been transformed into a genuine spiritual practice. This advanced spiritual love-making will never drain you energetically. In fact, it always gives you more energy. Making love like this raises your vibration, and the purified, but still fiery, sexual energy you generate can shoot your consciousness right up to heaven. At last, the sexual act has become truly satisfying to your core-self or soul. An instinctive human drive has been elevated into a pure expression of divine love and union.

Meditation

I am now prepared to let go of the pain and grievances from my past sexual relationships

Sit quietly and connect to the light.

Bring into your mind a past sexual hurt or grievance of some kind – but please do not try to heal child sex abuse issues or other major forms of sexual abuse without getting professional support.

Now ask your intuitive heart 'Am I now ready to let this past pain go?'

Gently tune into the pain of this past sexual hurt. Where does this pain manifest in your physical body? How does your heart feel when you tune into this sexual hurt? What stories do you tell yourself about this painful incident/relationship?

Now imagine letting all of this past pain and hurt float upwards, like a black ball of energy until it dissolves into a very bright light. If it helps use the mantra 'Letting go, letting go' as you do this.

As this past pain dissolves into the light, feel a sense of deep peace filling your whole being and give thanks for the miraculous healing that has taken place.

Chapter Nine

Awakened Dying

How Would You Like to Die?

I know that you still have a lot of worldly concerns, we all do, but I can assure you that your mortgage or your career will mean absolutely nothing to you when you are on your death bed. So why not give some attention now to what may happen to you when you die, so that you will be better prepared for this once in a lifetime experience? Why not ask right now, 'How would I like to die?'

Dying is the ultimate human challenge because we face losing absolutely everything; our loved ones, our body, our home and all of our possessions; the lot! So please do not wait until you are terminally ill to face all your fears about losing everything when you die. Face them now while you still have a real chance of releasing them.

From the highest spiritual perspective, living and dying are one continuous process. Whilst you are living in a physical body, you should practise the art of dying, and whilst you are dying, you should tune your consciousness into living in the light. When your body dies, you do not. After your physical body is no more, you will continue to exist in another realm of existence. When you no longer have a physical body, you will certainly still exist, but where will you go and what will you do? One thing for sure is that you will no longer have to worry about making a living, eating healthy foods or finding a sexual partner.

In the East, even non-practitioners tend to make some preparations for their death, and Buddhist practitioners traditionally place a lot of emphasis on the importance of dying well by dying in the light. But in the West, most people just try to push all thoughts of death out of their minds. You may be planning carefully for your retirement, but how much thought have you given to your death? Yet death and dying are such a crucial part of all our lives.

Your intellectual mind cannot tell you what will happen to you after you die, but I can assure you that basically, you will still be your same old self with all your familiar strengths and weaknesses. There is really no such thing as death, just one type of form changing into something else, so there is no need to be so afraid of your physical body dying. We all go from one type of world to another when we die, but as Ram Dass has reminded us, 'Death is absolutely safe. It's just like taking off a tight shoe!' After you leave your body behind, you can even keep your old name for a while if you want to. But I am afraid that you will no longer have a passport, or driving licence, to prove that it is really you.

If you keep examining death, particularly if you learn to contemplate on it in a high meditative state, you will eventually realise that death is not ultimately real. Pure consciousness never dies, but once the physical body loses all of its life-giving energy, the soul has to leave the lifeless body behind. If you keep raising your consciousness above the battleground of normal physical existence and really look into death, you will come to realise that you have already died many, many times. You have had many temporary lives in a physical form of some kind or another, and at the end of each one of them, you had to go through some type of physical death. You have probably had many violent deaths and hopefully some peaceful ones too.

Unless they are murdered or killed suddenly in an accident or armed conflict of some kind, most human beings have to become terminally ill and very weak, before their body dies. However, I no longer accept the collective version of death that assumes that it will be a horrendously painful and frightening process. In fact, I am now quite looking forward to dying as the last great adventure that I will have this lifetime.

I do not know exactly how I will die. However, I have prayed, 'Please let me die during meditation,' because that is when my consciousness is at its highest. I plan to still be relatively strong and pain-free when I die, so that I have all my wits about me, as I move on into another dimension of existence or merge back into the totality of Life Itself.

I am absolutely certain that if you include practising dying as an integral part of your awakening journey, dying can be a truly beautiful experience. Of course, I cannot promise you that you will die without any frightening sickness, weakness or pain, but I strongly recommend that you release as much of your inner darkness as you can whilst you are still hale and hearty, so that you can die in peace. If you do not do this, you may have to release a lot of nasty, dark energy and extreme fear in a very short space of time just before you die, such as during a six month period of dying from terminal cancer.

From a spiritual point of view, the positive side of dying slowly from a terminal illness is that when your body is physically and energetically extremely weak, you will no longer be plagued by so many physical desires and fantasies. So, if you are already an experienced spiritual practitioner, as you go through the dying process, you can focus all of your attention on forgiveness, unconditional love and connecting to the spiritual light. Then when you finally leave your body, you can experience a blissful state of pure love and peace, or feel attracted to an incredibly bright light that will guide you into a higher realm of existence.

During the normal dying process, your whole system will weaken, and so a lot of suppressed fear and anger will probably bubble up to be released. In the East, it is accepted that human beings tend to clear a lot of negative karma like this just before they die. In the West, we tend not to like to think about all of this when we are well. But we are all going to die at some point – or rather we are all going to go through the process of leaving our body and our personality-self behind at the end of this little lifetime as our consciousness moves on from this physical plane of existence to somewhere else.

I urge you not to wait until you are dying to heal your 'stuff'. This very day, do your absolute best to forgive everyone in your life who may have hurt you in some way, and do not forget to forgive yourself for any hurt or pain you may have inflicted on others. What if you die suddenly with no time to forgive anyone, not even yourself? Please do not risk this tragic possibility; practise the incredibly healing art of forgiveness now, while you still have the chance.

Tell others how much you love them now because you can never be absolutely certain that you are going to see them again in this lifetime. But always remember that we are all eternal beings. After someone you love dies, you can still send them unconditional love and light to support their consciousness as they continue their eternal homeward journey in another plane of existence.

Death Does Not Really Change Us

When most people die, it can be a big shock to them, as they find themselves without a physical body and away from 'home'. But basically, they stay the same person. The idea that on dying, we miraculously change from being a grumpy, fearful human being into a loving, joyful angel is just a comforting myth.

Basically, when our physical body dies, we are still exactly the same consciousness that we were when we were dwelling in a physical body.

I'm sorry, but after you leave your physical body, you won't suddenly become a lot wiser, kinder or even happier, just because your body and the physical world you used to perceive through your five physical senses have disappeared. Whatever you stored in your mind whilst you had a body will still be there.

For example, if you were neurotically self-centred and fearful while you had a body, you will be exactly the same without it. If you were very addicted to alcohol or cigarettes whilst you were in your physical body, you may even find yourself playing the role of a 'hungry ghost' after you die. Your cravings will still be there in your consciousness, but you will no longer have any way to satisfy them through your physical body, and so the pain and craving in your mind will be much worse.

You may find it hard to believe that you will be the very same self without your body, but please contemplate on this spiritual truth for a while. We do not say to one another, 'Your body is generous,' or 'Your body is intelligent'. We say, '*you* are generous,' or 'Y*ou* are intelligent'.

In fact, whatever qualities you acquire this lifetime, good or bad, will still be yours after your body dies. Of course, after you leave your body, you will have to adapt to a totally new environment in which you may well learn different lessons to this world's lessons, but your level of consciousness will still determine your perception of it. Someone who was extremely fearful, or maybe even paranoid for most of their life on earth, will not perceive themselves as being in a blissful, heavenly realm after they die, just as they did not experience a beautiful, loving world around them whilst they had a physical body.

Life is continuous, even though we seem to die and break that continuity. So if we become good at something in one lifetime, that innate capacity stays with us, and we can take it with us into another physical life, or even into a life in a higher realm of existence. On the other hand, if we accumulate some very bad habits in a particular lifetime, we will have a propensity to suffer from those same bad habits in our next life/dream of life. Then we will say to ourselves, 'That is so unfair! Why do I have to suffer like this? I never asked for this awful life.' But you are simply re-running a negative programme that was already in your individual consciousness.

Whenever you ponder on life after death, please remember this basic principle: *whatever you see around you always reflects what is in your mind, whether you are in a physical body or not.* A number of modern scientists are beginning to hint at this deep spiritual truth: reality is subjective, not objective. We hold certain beliefs in our minds, and then we project these beliefs outwards to create the external world around us. All I would add is that we do this whether we are in this physical realm of existence or some other realm.

If your consciousness is high enough after you leave your physical body, you can dwell in a much higher, celestial dimension of life that lies beyond physical time and space. You can move on to experience a heavenly state of existence or consciousness filled with blissful love and light. You will still have an individual consciousness, but this consciousness will be filled with divine love, without even a hint of conflict, hatred, fear or sorrow.

However, you will need to be a truly dedicated long-term spiritual practitioner who has already established an exceptionally strong connection to the light, to reach this very high level of consciousness after your body dies.

Ultimately, our individual consciousness can become so expansive that it merges totally with God or total oneness, and then the whole cycle of life and death is over forever. But please do not worry about totally losing your individual identity in this way. I very much doubt that it will happen to you in the foreseeable future, although, paradoxically, total enlightenment is always waiting for you in the Eternal Now beyond all time and space.

Practising Dying

All normal human beings, unless they are suicidally depressed, are instinctively afraid of dying. If we simply try to avoid facing our fear of death, or stuff it deep down into the subconscious layers of our mind, we will never overcome it. So we urgently need to awake and then connect to a spiritual light more and more strongly. This light can then assist us to dissolve all our fears, including our fundamental fear of dying. When children are afraid of the dark, we put a light on for them, and when we are afraid of death or dying, we need to turn on a spiritual light for ourselves and then use that light to illuminate all aspects of our fear of death until it completely dissolves.

If you learn to do this consistently whilst you are feeling relatively strong and radiant, you should still be able to do it whilst you are going through the dying process. But first, you need to practise the art of dying peacefully in the light. Each time you practise dying in your mind, you are cutting through another layer of your fear of death, until death completely loses its sting for you.

One of the difficulties we have with dying is that we can only do it once in a lifetime. Moreover, in modern secular societies, most people spend their whole lives in denial about death and dying. However, if we want to master this fundamental human challenge, we need to find some way of practising dying whilst our minds and bodies still strong. We need to become so familiar with the dying process that we are no longer afraid of it.

You can definitely prepare for your eventual death, whatever form it may take. Our minds can quite easily imagine dying in all sorts of different ways, such as drowning, being shot or wasting away from some kind of disease. But if we do not practise going through the dying process, fear of the unknown will probably overwhelm us when we die, and so we may not be able to die peacefully or gracefully.

Underneath our conscious mind is a deep, dark layer of extreme existential fear. Some people go unconscious when they die to protect themselves from this fear rising up in their minds. But then they completely miss the wonderful opening in our consciousness that occurs around the time of our physical death. Even just thinking about dying can bring up a lot of fear for most people, and extreme fear always makes us long to hide. This is why many people go unconscious when they die and thus miss a once in a lifetime opportunity to experience the spiritual light in all its non-physical brightness.

However, if we are brave and determined enough to practise the art of dying, we can learn how to connect to a much higher non-physical light or radiant energy long before we die. We can then rely on this well-established connection to the light to lift our consciousness upwards as we die. It can be extremely challenging to connect to the light when our bodies are very weak or in a lot of pain, but the more we practise connecting to the light while we are strong and healthy, the more it will sustain our consciousness throughout the dying process.

To die well, we need to be able to focus one-pointedly on the light whatever else is happening to us. So please do not be a fair weather practitioner. If you only practise connecting your individual consciousness to the light when you are feeling strong and vibrant, how likely is it that you will be able to connect to the light when you are dying? If, on the other hand, you keep practising through thick and thin, for example by meditating for 30 minutes or so each day even when you have the flu or when you are jet-lagged, you will stand a much better chance of sustaining your core spiritual practices throughout the dying process.

Once, several years ago in Thailand, I woke up in the middle of the night, feeling as though I was dying. I felt a massive electrical shock pulsing through me, and I truly believed that this shock was going to kill me. At the time, I tried to focus all my attention on the light, but I could not hold my focus 100 per cent. I also noticed that my heart centre was still not open enough to feel divine love bathing my whole being. So after that experience, which turned out to be just some kind of exceptionally strong energetic initiation, I practised dying a lot more diligently. I practised opening my heart to love and strengthening my connection to the light as I imagined dying, until I knew that I was fully prepared to die at any moment, if that was God's will for me.

Ways to Practise Dying

Rather than fighting against our fear of death, it is really helpful to learn how to surrender ourselves to the dying process. We are all paranoid about dying, but we undoubtedly have the potential to heal this deep fear 100 per cent.

One very simple way to do this is to practise dying every night as you drift off to sleep, because every night, you go completely unconscious for a while, and thus mimic the dying process. Each night just before you drift off to sleep, I recommend that you use a prayer such as 'I am dying in your arms Christ/ Buddha/Mother Mary/Kuan Yin, please hold me and protect me'. Then, simply practise surrendering to the light, as you let go into an unconscious state. Do this night after night, until the idea of dying no longer frightens you so much.

If you have already made an exceptionally strong connection to the light, you might also consider going through different deaths in a deep meditation. There is a lot of grief, hopelessness, guilt, fear and loss associated with dying, and as you practise going through different types of death, you can get in touch with many, many layers of unconscious darkness in your mind. Human beings have died in thousands of different ways and these experiences are now in our collective consciousness. So if we are brave enough and have a strong enough connection to the light, we can deliberately feel what different types of death are like, rather than choosing to ignore our fears about them.

We can use the power of our own minds to imagine going through all the stages of a plane crash, or a fatal car accident. We can imagine not being able to breathe as we drown in a stormy sea, or the sudden shock of being shot in the chest. On one of our healing courses, Jane practised experiencing being beheaded. At first she could not go all the way through the scenario she created in her mind. But after a few attempts, she managed to imagine actually having her head chopped off and then found herself laughing at the absurdity of still existing, but without a head!

However, imagining going through violent deaths like this a radical and pretty challenging meditative practice, so I strongly suggest that you start with practising dying peacefully. Just imagine that you are gently losing all of your energy or chi, until your body is lifeless and your consciousness peacefully soars out of your crown centre into the light.

When we are facing death, our untrained mind can play tricks on us and tell us that we are going to lose absolutely everything when we leave this world. Some people are so afraid of this loss that they cling onto their suffering bodies and cannot die peacefully at the appropriate time. However, if we can get in touch with an illuminated observer within, and utilise this observer to watch ourselves going through all kinds of deaths, this observer can assist us to overcome our fear of dying.

This illuminated observer knows that death is not real because all life is eternal. On the other hand, our lower minds do not experience this truth about life. Our egoic minds are always full of fear and paranoia about dying, and so we need to keep practising rising above our fearful, neurotic thoughts about dying. We also need to practise connecting ourselves to the all-knowing higher mind that is always dwelling in perfect love and peace, even during our body's death throes.

Another very helpful practice associated with dying is to imagine that you only have three days left on this earth. If you were to die in just three days' time, what would you regret not having accomplished this lifetime? I can assure you that you will not say to yourself, 'I wish I had worked harder so that I could have climbed up one more rung of the career ladder.'

However, there may well be someone in your life whom you have never told how much you love them. Or maybe you realise that there is someone whom you need to ask for forgiveness. You may also notice that you have not yet fulfilled your true purpose this lifetime. We all have a soul mission to fulfil this lifetime, and if we do not fulfil it, we will die with regrets.

What Happens After We Die?

When we die, our energetic vibration and level of consciousness will determine how conscious or unconscious we will be after we leave our bodies. If our vibration is high enough, we will quite naturally ascend to some kind of heavenly realm of existence. But if our consciousness is exceptionally low, we may experience being in a hell-like realm after we die, because we will no longer have a physical body to protect ourselves from experiencing all our worst inner fear, guilt and darkness.

The hell realms, or hellish states of consciousness, correlate to extremely low energetic vibrations. At its lowest, a hell realm can be experienced as a place of endless emotional torture and total fear, and the only way to get out of it is to pray ceaselessly for release. Hell is like an endless bad trip, a nightmare of epic proportions. It is certainly not a physical place full of fire and brimstone. But hell definitely exists as a state of consciousness that is extremely dark and agonising. All you can do if you find yourself in hell – and some individuals find themselves 'in hell' even whilst they still have a physical body – is to pray for mercy, until you finally experience some light that will rescue you from your own horrendous darkness.

If you just keep praying, even when your individual consciousness has sunk down to a hellishly low level, a little light will inevitably dawn into your awareness at some point, and then you can begin to rise up into a higher level of consciousness again. But my sincere advice to you is to practise diligently every day to raise your consciousness to the level at which there will be absolutely no chance of you descending into a hellish state of consciousness after your body dies.

After your physical body stops functioning, you will still have an astral body for a while. This body is made of a subtle chi-like energy which then gradually dissolves so that spirit or consciousness can move on into a higher astral world where you can learn new lessons. According to *The Tibetan Book of the Dead*, after you die, you can use this astral body to visit your loved ones.

Most people are unconscious – like being in a very deep sleep – for several days after they die, because some souls really need a rest or a break from the fear and trauma that they suffered during the dying process. But as they regain consciousness, they often visit their family and loved ones. It takes time to adjust to not having a solid physical body, but once you adjust to having an astral body, you can move this body with your mind, and thus travel to visit your loved ones, or tune into their thoughts and feelings.

So after a loved one dies, please be careful what you think or say about them, because your deceased loved one may be very psychic for a while, and will probably know what you are thinking and feeling about them. Most spirits will be curious about their funerals and what is happening to their physical bodies, and some spirits, who are particularly troubled or particularly attached to some place or someone on the physical plane, may even become earthbound after death. They may then become stuck in time and space and unable to move on. They are like the spirits in the film *The Others*.

However, if your consciousness is high enough, higher beings can definitely help you to move on from this world after you die. In the celestial realms, angelic beings have tremendous mercy and compassion for suffering beings in lower realms of existence, and they long to connect to those souls so that they can assist them to rise out of their suffering. Some angelic beings love to assist souls who have just left their physical bodies so that they can go up to a heavenly realm of existence for a while.

In this physical realm of existence, angelic beings will not hold your hand all of the time because they want you to grow spiritually. In this world, you cannot always be like a child who relies on a higher being to guide and look after them. You cannot lean on Jesus Christ or Buddha forever. Eventually, as you progress on your unique awakening and healing path, you have to grow up and become a Spiritual Master in your own right. Nevertheless, when you are going through the extreme challenge of physically dying, ascended masters and celestial beings will undoubtedly be there to assist you to reach a much higher level of existence, as long as you consciously choose to ask for their miraculous help and guidance.

So after you die, you may well experience a heavenly being or a heavenly light calling you to move on into a higher realm, or higher astral plane of existence. Gradually, as you adjust to living in this new world, you will forget about the physical forms of your loved ones and move on. But if you have unfinished business or karma to complete in the physical world, you may be quickly pulled back down into another physical form. Sometimes, we may even volunteer to go through another physical life so that we can learn some more lessons, clear some unfinished karma, or fulfil some kind of mission to help humanity.

After our body dies, we have an opportunity to see the true purpose of the life that has just ended much more clearly. But if we are not very awake or conscious, and do not have a strong internal observer, we can quickly be propelled by 'karmic winds' back into yet another physical existence. Karmic winds are not real winds, they are just a poetic description of jagged, unhealed internal darkness that can pull your consciousness in various directions and thus blow you about like a fallen leaf, until your consciousness falls back into another physical life.

Most human beings usually have quite shaky or chaotic consciousness and so they can very easily be blown about by karmic forces. Then, they may have to recycle their previous karma in a new physical life. Lifetime after lifetime, we meet members of our soul group again and again to repeat karmic cycles with one another. If we do not begin to awake, heal and forgive one another as we do this, we will simply repeat the same patterns in our lives over and over again, until we finally choose to become more conscious and much more forgiving of everyone's past mistakes.

Once your consciousness rises up to the level of 'love energy', you will have far more choice over where you go after you die than less conscious souls. You may dwell in a higher realm for quite some time, or you may volunteer to come back down to the physical plane in order to evolve further and/or to assist others to awake. This is what great Buddhist Lamas do when they die. They tend to reincarnate quite quickly as a selfless service to the world.

When an individual soul finally becomes enlightened, they do not have to have another physical existence in order to clear more karma. They can actually progress further through dwelling in higher realms of existence. However, some highly evolved beings do choose to lower their vibration so that they can come back down to earth, either to grow further through facing more worldly challenges, or simply to assist their suffering brothers and sisters.

Becoming Familiar with the Physical Process of Dying

As we die, it will be really helpful to raise our consciousness above the physical level so that we can detach as much as possible from our physical body. We should simply let our body do its own thing, without paying it too much attention. We can also begin to move on consciously from this physical world by placing our attention on higher realms of existence. Our aim is always to go to the highest possible level of consciousness we can reach, but we also need to be familiar with all of the physical sensations of dying so that they will not frighten us, or pull our focus away from the light as we die.

We cannot really rush the dying process. It has a momentum of its own and everyone will die in their own time and pace. Please understand that the physical body has its own elemental intelligence. There is a survival instinct built into all of its cells, and so sometimes the dying process can be rather long and drawn out because the body will try to cling onto life.

When the body is dying, all your earthly energy will gradually dissipate. First, your fire energy will go, and so your body will begin to feel cold and you will no longer be able to digest food. Next, the water element goes, and so you will feel dry and possibly thirsty. Then, the earth element disappears, and so you may feel floaty, and maybe confused, or even disorientated. Finally, when the air element goes, your breathing will probably become slow and laborious, and you may start to drift in and out of physical consciousness.

The key to a good death is to notice all of this without becoming overwhelmed by fear or anxiety. If you are determined to die a good death, I suggest that you practise feeling all of the above physical sensations so that they will not come as a shock to you, and frighten you to bits as you go through the dying process for real. For example, you can mimic your body feeling cold or heavy, and you can imagine your brain not working too well. You can also practise shallow breathing and making your in-breath shorter than your out-breath.

As you practise the art of dying, always remember to tune into the light to support your personal efforts to transcend the process of physical death. When the time actually comes to die, just pray for divine assistance, relax and focus on the light. Hold a loving intention at your third eye, and then allow the light to infuse your consciousness and envelop your whole being.

If you have any kind of spiritual community or sangha, ask them to pray for you and to hold the light for you as you go through the dying process. Spiritual practitioners and healers can create a powerful circle of light to support someone who is going through the process of dying, even if they do so from a distance. Also, when you are dying, ask someone to clear the energy in your room on a regular basis, because as we die, we can sometimes release a lot of inner darkness out into the atmosphere. Similarly, if you are helping a loved one to die, and you are an energy practitioner, keep clearing the room energetically to create a peaceful space around them.

As you die, if you focus one-pointedly on the light, you may even have a blissful experience. This may sound weird to you, but I assure you that your consciousness can be bathed in divine love and light as you leave your physical body behind and then your consciousness will expand greatly. This is an exceptionally good death. You lift your consciousness to a heavenly realm of existence and experience incredible amounts of bright light and blissful love as you gently and gratefully leave your physical body behind.

I would now like to describe for you at least two graceful ways to exit planet earth. One way is to deliberately weaken your body until it has no chi, for example by not eating anything, and then tuning into your soul as it gently withdraws from your chi-less body. If you are a high level spiritual practitioner, the energy of your soul can simply withdraw from your weak body very peacefully and naturally. But before you can die peacefully like this, you will have to have healed almost all of your inner pain and darkness, so that you do not die in fear and turmoil.

A much more dramatic way for a very advanced spiritual practitioner to leave their body is for them to open up to a blast of out-of-this-world high energy that can then shoot into their heart like a bolt of lightning. This 'bolt of lightning' can act like an energetic rocket to propel the advanced practitioner's consciousness out of their physical body and into a much higher realm of existence. But I need to warn you that you would need to be an exceptionally advanced practitioner in an incredibly high energy field to be able to do this.

Helping Others to Die Peacefully

As well as preparing for our own deaths, awakening souls may well find themselves being called upon to assist others to die well. If you find yourself in this position, extending human love that is tinged with fear and grief to the person who is dying is not enough. You need to be unafraid of death and have a very strong, powerful connection to the light, in order to be of real help to a friend or loved one as they die.

Everyone dies differently. There is no blueprint for dying, so please don't impose your ideas on how someone should die on a dying person who may not share your beliefs or level of awakening. Simply hold the light and peace for someone who is dying, and allow them to die in their own way. For example, don't read *The Tibetan Book of Living and Dying* to a committed Christian or Muslim as they are dying. Ask them instead if they would like you to play something they find uplifting, such as a favourite hymn, or piece of classical music, or whether they would like you to read to them from one of their favourite books.

When someone is dying, and they do not have any strong connection to a higher being such as Christ or Buddha, you may be able to help them to connect to their loved ones who have already passed over. If a dying person can connect to a loved one 'on the other side' as they die, they can definitely die in peace, even without any higher spiritual connection. So you can gently say to someone who is near to death, 'Don't worry about anything in this world. Think about your mother/father/sister/partner waiting to welcome you to Heaven.'

Many people who have had near death experiences have reported that they saw dead relatives waiting for them on the other side. Visions like this can really comfort the dying, and after such a vision, they may even yearn to leave their body so that they can be re-united with their lost loved ones. So if you are with a very close relative or friend when they are dying, be careful do not say anything to them such as, 'Please do not die. I can't bear to lose you.' Don't try to hang onto a dying loved one and do your best not to disturb them by getting distressed in their presence. Stay strong and calm whilst you are with them. You can always release your own grief and other painful emotions later.

I sometimes advise my students to practise some Infinite Tai Chi or Infinite Chi Kung, particularly *The Golden Sun Sequence*, near a person who is dying to clear any dark energy that may be being released through the dying process. If you know how to raise the energy in a room, a dying person can feel more supported in the light, and much safer in the calm, clear atmosphere that will surround them.

In non-practitioners, the dying process is often not a peaceful process until the last few moments, and so you need to practise clearing your energy and holding the light on a daily basis, until you are strong enough to hold the light for someone who is dying, without being disturbed by any agitation or dark energy that the dying person may be releasing.

Don't Waste Your Precious Time on Planet Earth

We all need to develop very consistent spiritual practices in order to transcend our fear of death and the process of dying. Most of us waste all of our lives pursuing pretty pointless worldly dreams, or getting caught up in endless worldly problems, and then death rushes in and takes us completely by surprise. If you commit to awakening, time can actually be kind and merciful, but if you waste your life away, time can become merciless, and before you know it your little life is over and you have achieved nothing of any lasting value.

Most people drift through life in a dream-like state. They get mired in their petty personal problems and then they drown in the fear and anxiety these worldly problems trigger in their minds. They suffer all their life from a deep sense of unworthiness or guilt, and then they die. They die without releasing any of their stored fear and guilt, and without having any real awareness of the true meaning of life and death.

Advanced spiritual practitioners, on the other hand, know without a shadow of doubt that death is not ultimately real. The enlightened state of being is deathless, and someone dwelling in this state can cover everything with the light, including the dying process. Dying without any fear whatsoever is still extremely rare in our world. However, if you can raise your vibration high enough during a meditation so that you can imagine watching your body dying, you can at least begin to realise that the dying process is just another dream that we all have.

I know the subject of death and dying is still not popular in our modern Western world. But what an amazing service you would provide for humanity if you became a pioneer of dying gracefully and even joyfully. How wonderful, if you could demonstrate to your fearful loved-ones that death is just another illusion. In any case, I confidently predict that sooner or later, the whole of humanity will awaken to this eternal truth: we are not just temporary physical beings born to die. We are eternal souls. We always were, and always will be, an integral part of Life Itself. There is therefore no such thing in ultimate reality as an end to our existence through physical death, only endless new beginnings.

Meditation

*I am not my body. I am an eternal being.
Physical death is not the end, but just another
new and exciting beginning.*

Sit quietly and connect to the light until you feel a deep sense of safety and security.

Now imagine your own funeral unfolding. See yourself looking down on your body in a coffin and experience the freeing sensation of still existing without being trapped in a physical body. See all your friends and loved ones attending your funeral and fill your heart with love and gratitude for them.

Now spend a few moments seeing, feeling or imagining blissfully warm love energy filled with brightness enveloping your whole being, as you gently open your heart and connect to the healing presence of Perfect Love. As you bathe in this healing presence, gently tell yourself, 'I am not a body. I am an eternal being'.

Chapter Ten
Awakened Living

Your Soul's Mission

After you awake, your life's purpose will change. Making a lot of money for its own sake, for example, will probably become far less important to you, and the core purpose of all your close relationships will change. But even after you awake spiritually, you should keep asking, 'Why am I living in this world? What is it all for? What is my purpose for being here?'

For me, physical life has no real meaning unless we can connect to our soul's true purpose. When I was young, I had no idea I was going to become a spiritual teacher and healer. When I was in my 20s, my life was all about 'me', and so I pursued activities I thought would bring 'me' security and pleasure. But after I awoke spiritually, everything changed.

What is your real purpose for being here? Please decide to search for a truly meaningful goal for your life and then keep going until you definitely find it, or when you reach your death bed, you will still be confused and disappointed with life. Most people are confused and disappointed all their lives because they have never discovered their soul's purpose for incarnating into a body this lifetime.

At every level of your growth, you will need to take a crucial decision. You will have to make a choice between living your life in fear and conflict and living your life in love and peace. However, once you genuinely commit to living the rest of your life in love, I can assure you that the whole universe will change to support your new choice. When you finally connect to your soul and make an unshakeable commitment to fulfil your soul's purpose this lifetime, your life-script will also change, sometimes quite dramatically.

Please do not just set yourself the goal of living in your current physical body as long as possible. What for? How many billions of individuals have lived on planet earth up until today? One thing they all had in common was that they all dropped dead incredibly quickly in the bigger scheme of things. Moreover, the vast majority of them never asked any deep questions about the meaning of life.

The true purpose of life is always to use your body to serve God/Love in your own unique way. Your body is basically just a vehicle, not an end in itself, and when it is serving a higher purpose, it will not die until it has fulfilled that purpose. When a body is serving the light, there is a bright energy surrounding and permeating it, so that it will not become too weak or even age that much. But you have to be an advanced spiritual practitioner for your body to be exceptionally radiant like this, and there are, as yet, very few shining examples of radiant spiritual masters in our world.

A really good way to think about our life on this earth is that we are all preparing ourselves to fulfil a mighty purpose. We keep learning life-lessons and raising our consciousness until we can embody the light and thus become a vehicle for the light to assist others through us. But before we can do this, we have to make a conscious choice to surrender to a higher plan for us, and sadly, most human beings are not yet awake enough to do this.

However, once you have established a really strong connection to the light, your soul will prompt you to help suffering humanity in some way. If you wish, you can do this by just sitting on a desert island, or in front of your living room hearth, meditating on love and light and then extending these divine qualities out into the world. When someone has a strong connection to the light, they naturally counteract some of the deep darkness in our world, whether they play an active role in world affairs or not.

But some awakened souls are not suited to a life of more or less constant meditation, prayer or contemplation, and so they pray to be guided to help humanity in a more active way. These souls will then be trained up by a much higher power who will guide them to develop all the particular skills and qualities that they will need this lifetime to become light-workers of one kind or another.

Fulfilling Your Soul's Purpose

Your soul has a unique purpose to fulfil this lifetime and you will never be truly content unless you honour it. Please understand that you can never just copy someone else's path or soul's purpose. You cannot be a Mother Theresa or Nelson Mandela clone. So, when you decide to follow your soul's purpose this lifetime, you are stepping into the complete unknown and therefore you will need some kind of guide to follow. This guidance may appear in your life as an external guru or teacher, and/or as an inner guide of some kind, and the best way to connect to your inner guide is to meditate on a very regular basis.

Meditation can really assist you to connect to your inner guide. Without a consistent meditation practice, you will inevitably keep getting lost in this chaotic world. But once you learn to meditate, you can really begin to rely on an inner guidance to direct all of your actions. Being able to connect to a higher, guiding power is crucial. Feeling a deep, spiritual impulse to act to help humanity in some way or another, is quite different from following what your personality thinks you should do, or listening to the crazy logic of the egoic thought system.

Personalities can claim to be spiritual, and they can even act in ways that may look as though they are helping others, but when we follow an egoic desire to look spiritual, or to feel good about ourselves by 'saving the world', we can often make some very painful mistakes. Unhealed healers and spiritual teachers can do a lot of damage in this world. For example, they can encourage child-like dependency on their magical powers and thus dis-empower the very individuals that they are claiming to heal or to enlighten.

A lot of very well-meaning individuals come up with plans to help others, but only a few are truly successful. Moreover, when highly intelligent, beautiful individuals finally solve a major problem in our world, such as eliminating Smallpox, another terrible scourge, such as AIDs, just seems to pop up from nowhere!

So please be patient and keep waiting until you know, without a shadow of a doubt, what your soul is meant to do this lifetime. Do not jump in prematurely and get it all wrong. Moreover, never assume that you know better than others how they should lead their lives. How arrogant it is to say to ourselves, 'I can fix this broken person,' or 'God needs my help to fix the world.' Really? I don't think so!

You have to awake before your soul's true purpose will be revealed to you, and sometimes you may have to keep waiting very patiently, until your consciousness rises high enough for you to have a clear picture of your spiritual mission this lifetime. You may already have developed some outstanding worldly talents, but you will not be able to fulfil your soul's purpose until you can connect to a much higher power that knows everything.

Your soul's gift is different from your worldly talents, although the two are usually linked. Your soul's unique calling can bridge the gap between heaven and earth. For example, Beethoven's later music was divinely inspired and thus embodies eternal, heavenly qualities.

When I first started giving spiritual talks, they were quite clumsy, but now when I am totally connected to a higher power, spiritual wisdom just flows through me effortlessly. I can also inspire large audiences with my performances of Infinite Tai Chi. But it took me many years of diligent training, and then many more years of learning to embody the light, before my Infinite Tai Chi Form sometimes moved people to tears.

As you grow and mature spiritually, your unique soul gift will also unfold and get stronger. But before you reach this advanced spiritual stage, you will need an awful lot of training and practice. As well as awakening, you also have to be very honest in evaluating your own worldly talents. For example, however divinely inspired you may be, you will probably not be an uplifting speaker, if you have a bad stutter.

Sometimes, our worldly talents may be there primarily to enable us to gather all the resources we will need to fulfil our spiritual destiny. For example, being a well-paid accountant or an IT expert may give us enough spare time and money to go to Thailand for a month-long spiritual retreat that most workers could not afford. We may also be blessed to earn large sums of money so that we can then sponsor others on their awakening, healing journeys.

But you also have to understand that what your personality-self wants may not fit with your soul's purpose or agenda. In fact, in my experience, the personality-self rarely gets all that it wants from pursuing some kind of spiritual path. Basically, your personality-self has no idea about your soul's purpose because the soul's agenda does not follow human reason or logic. But you do still have to use your personality's strengths and worldly charms to open doors and to build a 'spiritual business', if this is part of your soul's mission this lifetime.

For example, I combined my skills as a martial artist and tai chi practitioner with the fruits of my long-term meditation practice to set up spiritual training courses under the worldly guise of training Infinite Tai Chi teachers. Jane now uses several of the skills she honed during her long academic career to write spiritual articles and to give inspiring spiritual talks. It may look as though teaching, writing and public speaking come naturally to us, but we both spent many, many years practising certain core skills before we began to use them to fulfil our souls' purpose this lifetime.

Some spiritual seekers rather naively believe that if they surrender to God and agree to do spiritual work of some kind, God will provide them with all the resources they will need to be a huge success. But very often this simply does not happen. If we want to be both spiritually awake and successful in a worldly sense, we will still have to put a lot of our own effort and talents into building up a successful spiritual enterprise. Or we may first have to build up all the funds we will need, before giving up our paid employment to pursue a higher dream that does not pay well in worldly terms.

But do not wait too long to follow your heart. Some very well-meaning individuals tell themselves that they will just wait until the children are grown-up, or until they retire, to follow their spiritual path and then they realise that they have left it far too late to awaken and heal fully this lifetime. Their personality-self has basically sabotaged their soul's purpose.

If you wish to fulfil a higher spiritual purpose this lifetime, you will eventually have to relinquish your personality's very strong desire to control your future to gratify its own ends. Now, when I look back on my own spiritual journey, I can see it was all perfectly planned by a higher authority. But at times on my awakening journey, my personality-self still became quite frustrated by my apparent lack of progress.

Stop Playing Small

Some quite enlightened individuals in our society tend to play small. They may even adopt a rather fake form of humility that prevents them from shining their light out into the world. You may still say to yourself that you are just a normal human being, but I really do not recommend that you go on doing this. You cannot continue to play small and find true fulfilment in life. Once you have connected to the light, you have to commit to holding the light on behalf of others, and to do this, you have to honour your own unique, divine gifts as a child of God.

If you still believe that you are just a normal human being, you can only be helpful in this world some of the time, because whenever you are fearful, irritated, moody or judgemental, you will be part of the world's problem, rather than part of the solution. Please change your mind and see yourself as a fallen angel who has forgotten his/her true identity, rather than as a human being who is trying to become an angel. Mother Meera no longer believes that she is just a human being. She knows that her physical body is just a temporary tool to extend an incredibly powerful light out into the world. Going to see Mother Meera opened my eyes tremendously. She really inspired me to practise more, so that I could hold more light.

But if you are not yet ready to become a saint or an avatar, you can at least vow to 'reach the mountaintop' of human consciousness and thus become an exceptionally strong, abundant and helpful individual. To achieve all of this, you have to keep raising your vibration and consciousness. There is absolutely no point sitting around wishfully thinking your life could be better. Your life certainly won't change for the better unless you dedicate yourself to becoming the change you want to see in your life and in the world. You will not climb to the top of the mountain if you just keep sitting beneath it gazing up at it. At some point you need to put on your climbing gear and start climbing.

When you have raised your consciousness up to the mountaintop, you will still have an ego, but you will naturally become more compassionate, and you will begin to attract universal goodness and abundance into your life. You will become an extraordinary human being instead of a bog standard one! You will be radiant, and your radiant presence will be a true blessing in our troubled world. At this level of consciousness, you can even decide that you are ready to devote the rest of your life to selflessly serving humanity.

Dedicating your whole life to serving humanity is not about losing yourself or denying your personality's desires. It means finding your true-self beyond your little 'me' self that is always calculating 'What can I get out of doing this?' Great saints and spiritual masters, who always put others' interests above their own, are not really selfless. They are 'self-full'. Their consciousness has expanded into a higher truth in which they are no longer aware of any real difference between their needs and the needs of others.

When we begin to identify ourselves as a soul, rather than a personality-self in a body, we too will answer the universal calling to help humanity. But unless we link our very limited mind to a much higher intelligence that can work through us, helping humanity is really 'Mission Impossible'. Universal consciousness already knows everything – past, present and future – and so it can guide us every step of the way, as we devote our whole lives to selflessly serving suffering sentient beings.

In the East, they call selfless service 'karma yoga'. But Westerners tend not to understand this spiritual practice. Karma yoga is not about sacrificing our own needs in order to focus solely on meeting the needs of others. Truly serving others is never a chore or a sacrifice. As far as your soul is concerned, selfless service is true fulfilment. It may take you many years before you fully understand that selflessly serving others is a blessing rather than a sacrifice. Eventually however, you will just regard your egoic-self as a nuisance when it asks, 'What about me? What is in this for my benefit?' You will dismiss this sneaky egoic thought as a painful intrusion on your peace of mind.

Don't Just Want it. Will It!

Please don't just vaguely want to go out and spread the light in our troubled world. *Will* it. Connect to love energy and utilise its infinite power to guide you every step of the way. Spiritual will combined with love energy has real power behind it, but it does take quite a bit of mind training before you can use your higher mind to manifest your soul's purpose in this world. Willing your perfect future takes a very powerful mind focus and one-pointed commitment to making your highest dreams come true.

Once you master the art of spiritual willing, your whole life will unfold miraculously in front of your eyes. Even egoic will at least has a bit of power in it, compared to just wanting or fantasising. But spiritual will is much more effective because it involves joining forces with a higher power. For example, if you are looking for a new job or career, including a career as a light-worker, you can ask Jesus Christ, Buddha, Kuan Yin, or any other higher being, 'Please find the perfect job for me,' and they will be so happy to help.

Of course, higher beings do not actually look on the Web to find you the right employment opportunity. But once you join your small will to their mighty will, the energy field this true joining creates will increase your power of manifestation by a thousand fold – and then some. Moreover, when you ask higher beings to help you to manifest your highest dreams in this world, their energy will always work on behalf of the highest good of all concerned.

Egoic wanting is always weak because the ego can never truly join with others and therefore remains relatively powerless. But when you ask higher beings to join with you to create something for everyone's highest good, the world becomes your oyster. Your lower, thinking mind never knows how to get that dream job, perfect home or ideal partner, but higher beings always see a much bigger picture, and therefore know so much more. So whenever you need to manifest anything at all in this world, always tune into the power of the light, or the power of higher beings. If you do not do this, you are not being truly wise, however high your IQ may be.

Life always loves and supports you unconditionally, even whilst you are dreaming your life away. Therefore, when you spiritually will something for your highest good, and insist that, as God is your witness, you will succeed, you are affirming that it is a fait accompli. So please don't just long to become a successful light-worker, use a much higher will to manifest this miraculous future for yourself. Connect to love energy and know that your mission has already been accomplished.

I love to serve as many souls as possible, whilst I still have the physical strength to do so. I have now willed this to happen and

I know that this higher service will manifest perfectly. I also want to give generously to others to support their own awakening and healing, but I need greater resources to do this on any meaningful scale. I don't know the details yet, but I am certainly moving one-pointedly in the right direction.

I now trust that everything will work out for the best in ways that my individual mind cannot even begin to imagine. You may not have cultivated quite this level of trust yet, but trust is one of the most important qualities of a would-be miracle worker. So from this day forth, deliberately look for all the signs that your life is unfolding perfectly according to a much higher plan than anything your egoic mind could envisage.

Building Momentum

When you first start out on your spiritual mission, you will not usually be given a great big task to fulfil. You will be given smaller tasks, until you get stronger and more mature in the light. The universe is so kind like this. At first, you may be given some type of assistant light-working role, until you mature and are willing to take on a starring role. But you do need to do something to build the momentum. So if you want to selflessly serve humanity, why not begin by volunteering to assist, or support, a much more experienced light-worker in some way?

You definitely need to train yourself up to become a genuinely helpful spiritual presence in this world. So my advice to you is to follow some kind of long-term training programme, or specific spiritual path, so that you know where you are going. Don't flit about from one type of spirituality to another. Don't be a Buddhist one week and a Yogi the next. It takes many years to deepen into any genuine spiritual teachings and practices. You need to put a lot of time and effort into mastering any skill in this world, including core spiritual practices, such as meditation.

Following higher guidance is not simple, because at first, our ego keeps getting in the way. So we have to go through a lot of trial and error, as we learn to distinguish the voice of God or Spirit from the voice of the ego. It usually takes many years, if not decades, before a genuine practitioner can clearly distinguish higher guidance from egoic guidance and true love from egoic neediness.

Joining together for a higher spiritual purpose is not about joining our personality to other personalities in some kind of egoic alliance. We have to join with God or the Truth, so that we can transcend all petty personality squabbles and differences. We need to align with the light, and then join with others in the light, rather than in a fearful, self-centred egoic alliance.

Joining together to help our brothers and sisters is a great art. It takes time to really understand what it means to join with something much higher than you before you join with others, because to start with, you simply do not perceive the truth about life, you perceive mainly illusions. But eventually, if you persist, you will be ready and able to form a 'circle of. light' with other like-minded spiritual practitioners, and thus join together to follow a higher calling or cause.

Selflessly Serving Others

Never go out into the world to work primarily for your own benefit. Always go out to serve God, or if you do not feel comfortable with the word God, to serve Love. However, you do need to understand that working for God is a very new profession in our world, and so you may need to take some time to learn the ropes.

How can you follow your inspiration and know that you are on the right track as you go out to selflessly serve the world? First of all, if you are going to join with others to create a wonderful spiritual enterprise, such as a meditation centre or a healing course, you need to set aside all thoughts of self-profit or self-promotion and vow to put others' highest benefit before your own self-centred concerns.

As 21st Century spiritual entrepreneurs, I suggest that we now need to cultivate a co-operative spirit in which we join together with others in the light, and continuously put aside all our petty egoic grievances and disputes. If we do not keep doing this, it is so easy to end up hating each other when a joint spiritual venture, started with the best intentions, does not go according to plan.

Joining together with others is always powerful, but first, we do have to examine our motives for joining together with others in any kind of venture – even a so-called spiritual one. Are we joining together in an unholy egoic alliance, or in a holy alliance based on surrendering all our unhealed, self-centred, egoic concerns to a higher power?

Second, you should learn to act spontaneously in 'the power of now'. Of course, in this world, we do need to use some kind of reason or logic to plan ahead. We need to use our thinking brains to book venues for retreats and the travel tickets we will need to get to them. But we also need to have the courage to follow a heart-centred impulse as it rises up in the present moment. So please don't try to control or worry about your future spiritual career. Just stay in the power of now, so that you can answer the call from the divine when the timing is just right.

When I was younger, I really wanted an unmistakable sign of the path I was supposed to follow before I gave up my restaurant business to become a spiritual teacher. But this sign never came. Eventually, I realised I just had to keep bringing myself back to the present moment and then act spontaneously. At that time, I did not know that I could open my heart and then simply follow an infinite wisdom that would make itself known to me as a heart-centred knowing or intuition. But I did know that I was being called to do something other than be a successful businessman. So I reluctantly walked away from my profitable business and began to 'spread the light' through teaching Infinite Tai Chi and Infinite Meditation.

Third, when you commit to serving others in some way or another, you need to cultivate persistence. I have noticed that some of my spiritual friends are sporadically inspired to do something to serve others selflessly, but then they lack persistence. Moreover, I have witnessed a number of very genuine, spiritually inspired individuals going out to teach or to heal others, without being fully trained to do so. Unfortunately, they made lots of unskilful mistakes, and some ended up broke and depressed. So please do not be naïve and think that if you set yourself up as a spiritual teacher or healer, God will perform miracles on your behalf. God is not some great magician in the sky who will shower gold coins down on you to reward you for following some kind of spiritual calling.

You actually need a lot of challenging and disciplined training before you will be able to stay centred in love, light and peace in this chaotic world, regardless of the mayhem going on all around you. Cancer cells for example, are very dark and nasty, and I certainly would not advise any of my Ling Chi Healing students to offer a healing to someone with cancer, before they had completed several years of advanced Ling Chi Healing training. Similarly I do not advise my Infinite Tai Chi graduates to go and teach The Infinite Arts in extremely challenging environments such as prisons, unless they are exceptionally energetically, physically and emotionally strong and resilient.

Finally and crucially, you need to keep connecting to the inspiration and wisdom of the light day in and day out. It is no good feeling inspired by the light on Monday and totally uninspired and burnt out by Saturday. You need to re-inspire yourself on a more or less daily basis because the more you become consistently inspired, the more you will be able to rise up above your egoic 'What about me?' thoughts, to shine out like a particularly bright star in our relatively dark and gloomy world.

When you go out into the world to spread the light, it may look to others as though you are doing perfectly normal work. But in your mind, you know that you are working only for God, or for Love. You will still need to cultivate worldly skills and experiences, but your core intention will be totally different to someone who is still working primarily for themselves and their own family.

What are the perks of working for God? For example, can you still have a really nice company car or a big occupational pension? A lot of spiritual practitioners are afraid to ask God for worldly things. But I strongly recommend that you ask God for everything, because infinite abundance is your spiritual birthright. In my experience, working for God does not mean that you have to die and go to heaven before He rewards you for your selfless service. Why not work for God and ask Him for a brilliant remuneration package? God could not care less what sort of worldly trimmings you have in this dream world. So why on earth do you not insist on having it all?

A higher wisdom, or light, can look after every aspect of your life for you in minute detail, including giving your personality-self wonderful treats from time to time. But first, you have to learn to trust this higher power absolutely. Just keep praying for your life to unfold perfectly for everyone's highest good, until you establish complete faith you will be looked after beyond your wildest dreams. Why do you insist on struggling with your work, your health, your relationships or your finances? Ask the light to assist you to heal all of your negative programming in these core areas of your life, and then insist on leading an exceptionally happy and fulfilling life until the day you die.

Many modern day spiritual seekers still believe that they have to sacrifice material abundance to follow their heart's joy or to serve others selflessly. But you absolutely do not have to do this. The lower, negatively programmed mind will say, 'If I go for completing my soul's higher purpose this lifetime, I will struggle financially.' Please don't think like this. Vow that you will be both spiritually fulfilled and infinitely abundant in this world. At the moment, a rogue plumber can earn a lot more than a genuine spiritual teacher or healer. This really is not on, and so we urgently need to become pioneers in changing the collective belief that genuine spiritual practitioners should not have much money.

Before you completely merge back into infinite, eternal oneness, please do your very best to create a really comfortable and enjoyable worldly existence for yourself. Watch the fabulous film *Michael* in which John Travolta plays an angel paying a brief visit to earth and revelling in the physicality of this world and learn a wonderful lesson from it.

I would also advise you not to give up paid employment prematurely to become a self-employed light-worker. We all need to earn some money in our modern world, and it takes time to really trust that God will provide for all our needs. However, it is true that some souls do eventually have to leave their day jobs behind so that they can fulfil their spiritual purpose this lifetime, even if they are really scared about how they are going to earn their living as they do so.

As you awake more and more, your soul's agenda will definitely begin to override your personality's agenda. When you are awake, you may find that you just have to fulfil your soul's purpose, regardless of your personality's fears around earning money, or moving to a different part of the world. When your soul awakes and is ready to do God's work in this world, you may well feel compelled to go out into the world as a spiritual healer, teacher or counsellor of some kind, even if to begin with you do not attract many paying customers. You may not realise it, but if you feel a strong calling like this, your clients or students may already be waiting for you to say a big unconditional 'Yes' to fulfilling your soul's true purpose this lifetime.

One of my Infinite Tai Chi colleagues was earning a lot of money selling beauty products, but she knew in her heart that she just had to become a full-time Infinite Tai Chi teacher and Ling Chi healer. At first, when she finally took the plunge and left her very well paid employment, she faced a lot of challenges, including facing her fears around money, but after a while, she learned to trust more, and the money to support her new life started to flow in. Moreover, those individuals who were just waiting for her to commit to her true purpose before they could begin their own awakening and healing journeys have now become her long-term students and healing clients.

Remember, when you answer the eternal call, you are never alone. If there are some aspects of a spiritual venture you know that you cannot do, such as accounting or marketing, just ask for the right person to be sent to assist you. If you need a bigger income to keep going as a light-worker, pray for the extra income to come your way. Always bear in mind that you are never asking life for too much, you are playing small and asking for too little. Keep asking for more love, more light, more miracles. Pray sincerely and unselfishly for abundance, and watch it manifest effortlessly right in front of your eyes.

If you face a few challenges along the way, as you establish a new spiritual career for yourself, don't give into fear and doubt.

Just give thanks for these wonderful opportunities to strengthen your faith in a beneficent universe. If you are rushing to get to an appointment that may open up a wonderful light-working opportunity for you and you get stuck in a traffic jam, have faith that in some inexplicable way it is perfect for you, and give thanks for it.

Jane was flying off to run a retreat in Spain recently when her plane was delayed for several hours. Then the airline staff announced that everyone was being sent to a Hilton hotel for lunch and would be brought back to catch the delayed flight that afternoon. But Jane trusted an intuitive inner voice that said 'Don't go'. To cut a long story short, twelve hours after they arrived at the airport, Jane and 19 other individuals were flown down to Gatwick on a specially commissioned empty plane and then flown onwards to Malaga to arrive late that evening, whilst 300 other delayed passengers had to wait until 2am the following morning to catch their flight. Jane then got a good night's sleep and started her retreat with a heart full of gratitude for her truly miraculous escape from Manchester Airport the previous day.

When you set your intention, pre-determine your destination, and then join forces with a much higher power in your prayers and meditations, everything that then happens to you will be assisting you to release all inner and outer obstacles to attaining your final goal. Please adopt this miraculous view of life. See everything that happens to you as working for your highest good, including redundancy, bankruptcy, divorce and even a life-threatening illness.

Don't Be Afraid of Challenging Times

As you go out to be a light-worker, don't be too afraid of facing worldly or spiritual challenges. Tough challenges on the path can really assist us to grow and to cultivate unshakeable strength and trust in life. Has anyone experienced spiritual growth, or a successful spiritual career as a genuine light-worker, without experiencing any hardship? It seems not. I have never heard of anyone just blissing out in love and light and fulfilling their highest purpose this lifetime with no effort at all. All of my students appear to go though many trials and challenges to assist them to become more empowered in the light. Some have gone through painful divorces or bankruptcies before becoming light-workers and one or two have even been through incredibly frightening psychotic breakdowns as part of their spiritual unfoldment.

When you go out into the world to serve others selflessly, it can definitely feel like hard work at times, and you will undoubtedly face many unexpected challenges, but these apparent obstacles on your path will only make you stronger. The light cannot do everything for you. It cannot magic you fearless and radiant. Your core-self has to keep challenging your personality-self so that you can continue to grow ever stronger. We actually create our own challenges on the path because our soul knows just how much these challenges push us to heal and to grow more radiant in the light.

The really good news is – despite all of the challenges you will face along the way – the more you commit to helping others, the more miracles just have to happen through you, and you will simply witness them over and over again. When you are in a very high energy field, it will seem as though you can perform miracles. But in reality, you have just moved your egoic-self out of the way so that miracles can happen through you.

The very best addiction that you can have in this world is to become addicted to experiencing inner peace, freedom, true love and joy, and then watching miracles happen as you extend unconditional love and light to others. Once you have tasted infinite love in a deep meditation, all other worldly joys will diminish in colour and flavour. Will doing God's work earn you a Ferrari, a Porsche, or a designer watch? You will not really care! How can driving a Ferrari or wearing a Rolex possibly compare to the abiding comfort of dwelling in infinite love and peace?

Your soul does not care about all the worldly trimmings that you may still value. True happiness has nothing to do with material wealth, or worldly fame and fortune. Perfect fulfilment in this life comes from dwelling constantly in peace, love and light and then extending all of these aspects of divine reality out to others. When your soul is totally free and fulfilling its highest purpose this lifetime, you will feel completely whole, with no desires or worldly cravings whatsoever. This is as close as we can get to perfection whilst still living in an imperfect world.

However, please do not pretend that you no longer care about material pleasures or comforts, if you still do. If you still want luxurious worldly experiences, as well as a career working for the light, pray sincerely for them and then say a big 'Thank You' for all the miraculous gifts that come your way. Whatever you do, do not feel guilty when something good happens in your life. If you find yourself running a retreat in a luxury hotel with staff catering to your every whim for a while, don't feel guilty. Feel truly grateful! Fill your heart to bursting with gratitude and joy.

Do you know that deep down you are afraid that God will take everything away from you to punish you for your sins? You start to become successful as a light-worker of some kind, and then you sabotage your success because you do not truly believe – consciously or subconsciously – that you really deserve to earn good money doing something you love to do. This is egoic paranoia at its destructive best.

God has already given you absolutely everything. Don't bargain with God. Just keep expressing your sincere gratitude for all of His Gifts. Say 'Yes' to all God longs to give to you and then say 'Thank You!' I repeat, you always ask God, or the light, for far too little, rather than too much.

However, please don't become too attached to worldly goods or experiences, or they will only bring you pain in the long run. If you run a yoga course in a 5* luxury hotel one year, don't insist on the same standard of accommodation the next year, or you will set yourself up to be disappointed. Just keep trusting God, and giving thanks for everything that He gives to you, even if it is only rather basic accommodation with only so-so food.

Becoming Miracle-Minded

Miracles are happening all around us all of the time, but most people are too caught up in their victim-like mentality to be able to notice the miracles occurring right in front of them. Why do you keep worrying about life so much? It is such a destructive habit! Of course, it does take an awful lot of training to be miracle-minded at all times, because our personality-self is always doubtful and fearful. However, with a lot of mind-training, and by raising your vibration and connecting more and more to your soul, you can begin to override your egoic-self to dwell in 'miracle-mindedness'.

When you are serving others in any capacity, watch out for egoic selfishness rearing its ugly head. The egoic thought system always goes something like this: 'If I wash your cup as well as mine and you do not return the favour, I will lose out.' Karma Yoga means washing other peoples' cups with love and joy, rather than any kind of resentment or judgement. But this takes time to cultivate. Only a few of my students love doing karma yoga, and even some of my most advanced students still suffer moments of resentment whilst serving others. Most affluent Westerners still expect to be served rather than to serve, even on a spiritual retreat.

The Dalai Lama is still selflessly serving his people and the whole of humanity, even though he is well past retirement age. But most people have a lot of resistance to selfless service because the egoic thought system insists that we should get something out of everything that we do. The ego always calculates 'What can I get out of this situation/person?'

In modern Western societies, we are all socialised into adopting a pretty self-centred point of view as we grow up. We are led to believe, for example, that we have an absolute human right to pursue our own individual happiness. We also expect to be rewarded for any service that we may provide for others. But the rain does not ask for payment when it gives us water, and the sun does not shine only on those who show their appreciation for sunny weather in some way or other. So now, as an advanced soul, you need to learn how to give selflessly, naturally and indiscriminately like the sun and the rain, without expecting anything in return from those whom you serve.

If you want to be truly fulfilled in life, earning money should never be your priority or your main motivation for providing a service to others. Nor should you serve others with the secret egoic motivation of wanting to be needed or admired. Just serve others with love and joy in your heart, and then give thanks when money or gratitude comes your way. Serving others selflessly will make you incredibly abundant in all sorts of ways. So always give thanks for any miraculous opportunity to serve others in some way, and revel in the feeling of abundance that giving to others will induce in you.

Once you completely align with your true-self, you will naturally long to give everything to everyone, with no thought of personal reward. Until then, you can enhance your service to others by devoting all of your actions to a higher power. For example, don't just wash other people's dirty dishes mindlessly. Wash them with true love and devotion. See yourself as washing a mug for Jesus or Buddha. This will counteract any tendency you may still have to feel resentful when serving less than perfect human beings!

Keep doing everything for love and in love and you will not go far wrong. Go out to work and earn good money by all means, but always dedicate your work to love itself. Whenever you are serving others, even a cat or a dog, know that you are serving God. Keep doing this day after day and, sooner or later, you will have to attain full enlightenment, because the path to enlightenment is the path of selfless love and service.

Once you connect to the awesome power of this love, nothing in the whole universe can possibly prevent you from fulfilling your soul's 'Mission Impossible' this lifetime. Nothing can stop you becoming part of a miraculous solution to the world's endless suffering, rather than just another helpless and tiny part of the problem.

Meditation

I am here to be truly helpful.
I am joining with all of my brothers
and sisters in love and light.

Sit quietly, tune into your breath and connect to a higher light.

Now use the power of your creative mind to see yourself sitting in the most beautiful garden you can possibly imagine. The sun is shining, the flowers are blooming, the birds are singing and a fountain of crystal clear water rises up from a small lake right in front of you.

See yourself sitting in a meditative position and then see, feel or imagine a very bright light extending outwards from your open heart centre.

Gently centre in your compassionate heart and then silently call all of your dear friends and loved ones to come and join you in your garden of love. See them being pulled into your garden by the power of the light emanating from the core of your being.

As your friends and loved ones join you in your garden of love, a deep feeling of infinite joy and peace envelops each and every one of you. You then sit together in a circle of light that gently, but powerfully, extends outwards to illuminate and bless the whole of Planet Earth.

Books, DVDs and Audio CDs Available

For further information and to order any book, DVD or audio CD listed below, please visit **www.lightfoundation.com**

Additional products, audio downloads, video downloads and on line courses are available from **www.theinfinitearts.com**

Other Books by Jason Chan

Seven Principles for Radiant Living, Jason Chan

Other Books by Jason Chan and Jane Rogers

The Radiant Warrior, Jason Chan with Jane Rogers
Infinite Abundance, Jason Chan and Jane Rogers

DVDs featuring Jason Chan

Infinite Tai Chi for Beginners
Infinite Tai Chi for Health
Infinite Chi Kung for Health

Audio CDs featuring Jason Chan

Infinite Meditation
Seven Stages to Spiritual Enlightenment
Whole Life Journey for Abundance